THE CAPE WRATH TRAIL

About the Author

Iain Harper lives and works in the Cotswolds, but has been walking in the Scottish Highlands for 20 years. He first discovered the Cape Wrath Trail in 2007 and since then has walked it many times researching this book.

THE CAPE WRATH TRAIL

by Iain Harper

2 POLICE SQUARE, MILNTHORPE, CUMBRIA LA7 7PY
www.cicerone.co.uk

© Iain Harper 2013
First edition 2013
ISBN: 978 1 85284 667 1

A catalogue record for this book is available from the British Library.

Printed by KHL Printing, Singapore

All photographs and illustrations are by the author unless otherwise stated.

For Angela, Tony and Kay

Advice to Readers

Given the march of time and the changing nature of the physical and human landscape, no printed guidebook can stay fully up-to-date for long, and changes can occur during the lifetime of an edition. If we know of any, there will be an Updates tab on this book's page on the Cicerone website www.cicerone.co.uk), so please check before planning your trip. We also advise that you check information about such things as transport, accommodation and shops locally. Even rights of way can be altered over time. We are always grateful for information about any discrepancies between a guidebook and the facts on the ground, sent by email to info@cicerone.co.uk or by post to Cicerone, 2 Police Square, Milnthorpe LA7 7PY, United Kingdom.

Additionally this guide works in tandem with a new website, www.capewrathtrailguide.org, where regular route news and updates will be posted. The site also allows you to share your own expedition reports, photos and videos for others to read as well as a comprehensive directory of accommodation and useful links.

Front cover: Approaching Ben More, Assynt

CONTENTS

Acknowledgements

Any book that follows a route primarily suggested by others inevitably owes a large debt of gratitude to those that blazed the trail. In particular David Paterson, Cameron McNeish, Denis Brook and Phil Hinchcliffe: without their pioneering and inspirational work, this route wouldn't be as popular as it is today. I'm very grateful to my beautiful and long-suffering wife, who put up with me being far away from home over two consecutive Christmases and many other trips to research this book. I'd also like to thank Bob Smith for his companionship during the second winter expedition where we endured some of the coldest conditions in twenty years. Tom Forrest has probably done more than any single individual to promote the Cape Wrath Trail and has been hugely generous with advice and support during the writing of this book. Thanks also to the many people who got in touch from all over the world with information fresh from their own journeys along the trail, in particular Dean Crosby and David Hird.

Overlooking Loch Hourn (Stage 4)

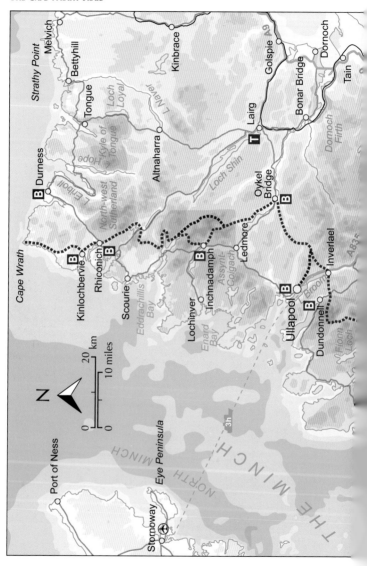

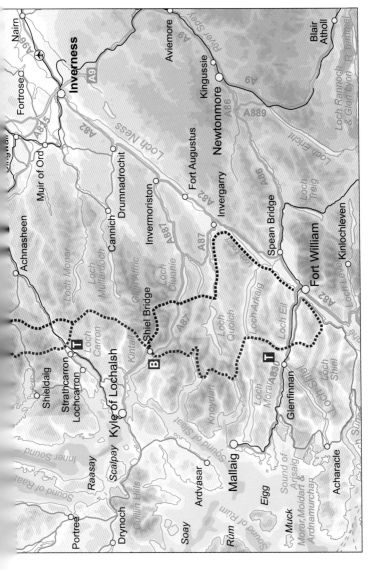

9

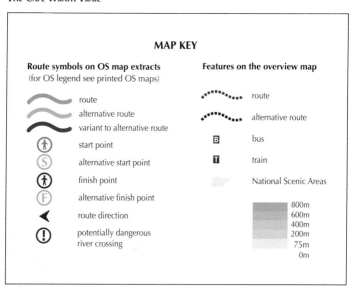

MAP KEY

Route symbols on OS map extracts
(for OS legend see printed OS maps)

route

alternative route

variant to alternative route

start point

alternative start point

finish point

alternative finish point

route direction

potentially dangerous
river crossing

Features on the overview map

route

alternative route

🅱 bus

🆃 train

National Scenic Areas

800m
600m
400m
200m
75m
0m

Warning

Mountain walking can be a dangerous activity carrying a risk of personal injury or death. It should be undertaken only by those with a full understanding of the risks and with the training and experience to evaluate them. While every care and effort has been taken in the preparation of this guide, the user should be aware that conditions can be highly variable and can change quickly, materially affecting the seriousness of a mountain walk. Therefore, except for any liability which cannot be excluded by law, neither Cicerone nor the author accept liability for damage of any nature (including damage to property, personal injury or death) arising directly or indirectly from the information in this book.

To call out the Mountain Rescue, ring 999 or the international emergency number 112: this will connect you via any available network. Once connected to the emergency operator, ask for the police.

PREFACE

Sandwood Bay (Stage 13)

After gazing at the sky for some time, I came to the conclusion that such beauty had been reserved for remote and dangerous places, and that nature has good reasons for demanding special sacrifices from those who dare to contemplate it.

Richard E Byrd, Alone (1938)

From the headland that juts imperiously over the broad ochre strand of Sandwood Bay, you may catch a first glimpse of the Cape Wrath lighthouse peeking over the low, dun hills of the horizon, beckoning you the final few miles towards the end of one of the world's finest long-distance walks. You'll already have crossed most of the northwest coast of Scotland via Morar, Knoydart, Torridon, Assynt and Sutherland, winding through some of its most remote and beautiful glens. Cape Wrath itself, staring out into the white-capped North Atlantic, closer to the Arctic Circle than London, is now within a day's walk.

The Cape Wrath Trail is not an officially recognised UK National Trail. In truth, it is not really a trail at

Descending into Gleann Cuirnean (Stage 2)

all, more a jigsaw of routes between Fort William and the most northwesterly point of the UK, to be assembled according to your preferences. Perhaps because of this unique flexibility and lack of formal status, it has become highly regarded by many backpackers. It's a tough test for anyone and you'll brave remote country, rugged terrain, rain, wind, midges, bog and tricky river crossings. Most people take between two and three weeks to complete the full journey and whatever time of year you attempt the trail it will test the limits of your physical and mental endurance. But dark, boggy moments are quickly forgotten amid a solitude and beauty rarely found in modern life.

This trail has an intriguing capacity to draw people into some of the most wild and remote places Scotland has to offer. The cape itself, so aptly named, pulls you inexorably northwards – there can be few other long distance paths with such an inspiring finale. There is also something in the challenge of traversing such a vast, primal and largely unspoilt tract of land that explains why this route has attracted so many fans. Its beauty lies in its freedom: you'll find few signposts around here. This one's for true connoisseurs of the wild lands, and it's down to you.

This book draws together updates and attempts to improve on a variety of routes that have previously been suggested. It also offers a wide range of variations, recognising that there can be no definitive path suitable for all. It shares the same intrinsic aims as those that have gone before, namely to visit the most scenic areas and avoid most tarmac roads and high level mountain traverses. This brings the route well within the abilities of most ambitious but experienced hill walkers.

The trail traditionally begins in Fort William and winds across Ardgour towards Glenfinnan, taking in the gloriously remote rough bounds of Knoydart before striking north to Shiel Bridge, Strathcarron, Kinlochewe and Inverlael, near Ullapool. A popular alternative route leaves Fort William via the Great Glen Way before turning north to cut across Glen Garry and Glen Shiel, rejoining the main route at Morvich, near Shiel Bridge. North of the Ullapool road, the route turns inland to Oykel Bridge before heading towards Glencoul via Inchnadamph and the majestic Ben More. Then, below the shadows of Arkle and Foinaven, the final stretch passes Rhiconich and on to the farthest northwest coast and over the moors to Sandwood Bay and the Cape Wrath lighthouse, the end of the journey.

Follow as much or as little of the route as you like. Take detours, plan alternatives, make the journey to the Cape your own. It's one that will live with you for the rest of your life.

Iain Harper, 2012

Path by Carnach River, Sgurr na Ciche in the background (Stage 3)

INTRODUCTION

The Cape Wrath Trail is part of a vast network of 720 long distance paths that criss cross the British Isles. Some of these are official National Trails – well maintained long distance footpaths and bridleways administered by Natural England and the Countryside Council for Wales and waymarked with acorn symbols. In Scotland, the equivalent trails are called Long Distance Routes and are administered by Scottish Natural Heritage. There are currrently 15 such routes in England and Wales and four in Scotland. Many other long distance paths are equally well maintained and waymarked. The Cape Wrath Trail is fairly unique, combining a complete lack of way-marking and a variety of routes rather than a firmly fixed trail. The route often follows traditional drovers' and funeral routes, dating back hundreds of years, that provided the only means for crofters to move themselves and their animals around the rugged landscape of the Scottish Highlands.

The route as we currently know it has evolved more recently, with landscape photographer David Paterson's 1996 book *The Cape Wrath Trail: A 200 mile walk through the North-West Scottish Highlands* setting out a basic template. Paterson set off from Fort William with his camera and a bivvy

View back to Glenfinnan (Stage 2)

Climbing towards the Forcan Ridge (Stage 4)

bag and his route was initially along the Great Glen Way, hence its inclusion in this book as a route alternative. The route starting along the Great Glen Way was further popularised by Cameron McNeish, wilderness backpacker and editor at large of *The Great Outdoors* magazine, who suggested a more practical and less circuitous alternative to Paterson. McNeish has included this version of the route in his Scottish National Trail, which spans the entire country. He neatly summarises the trail: 'It's the sort of long distance route that most keen walkers dream of. A long tough trek through some of the most majestic, remote and stunningly beautiful landscape you could dare imagine. The Cape Wrath Trail is a challenging and

often remote route which, in essence, could be described as the hardest long distance backpacking route in the UK.' A later book, *North to the Cape* by Denis Brook and Phil Hinchcliffe, cemented the trail's burgeoning popularity, and first suggested starting the trail through Knoydart rather than the Great Glen, a route that has now become firmly established as the more popular choice with walkers.

Because of its difficulty and the relative lack of amenities, the Cape Wrath Trail has resolutely defied the commercialisation that has come to other long distance backpacking trails in the Highlands like the West Highland Way.

More recently, the trail has become part of the International

Appalachian Trail (IAT), a backpacking trail running from the northern end of the Appalachian Trail in Maine, USA through New Brunswick, to the Gaspé Peninsula of Quebec, Canada after which it extends to Nova Scotia, Prince Edward Island, Newfoundland and Labrador. Geological evidence shows that the Appalachian Mountains and the mountains of Western Europe and North Africa are parts of the former Central Pangean Mountains, made when minor supercontinents collided to form the supercontinent Pangaea more than 250 million years ago. With the break-up of Pangaea, sections of the former range remained with the continents as they drifted to their present locations. Inspired by this evidence, efforts are being made to further extend the IAT into Western Europe and North Africa.

GEOLOGY AND WILDLIFE

This book is a walking guide not a natural history guide, but suffice to say that if you're a fan of rocks and creatures, you're in for a real treat. Assynt in particular has been described as an 'internationally acclaimed geological showpiece' and you're as likely to bump into a geologist as a stag wandering through its glens. You'll also be spoilt for choice with fauna, from the golden eagles of Knoydart, ptarmigan, red deer, a vast array of birds and even the odd seal in the western sea lochs. One of the best books

Descending to Loch an Nid (Stage 7)

on this subject is *Hostile Habitats – Scotland's Mountain Environment: A Hillwalkers' Guide to Wildlife and the Landscape* by Mark Wrightam and Nick Kempe. If geology is more your thing, then *Hutton's Arse: 3 Billion Years of Extraordinary Geology in Scotland's Northern Highlands* by Malcolm Rider is well worth a look, and not just for the fantastic title. Finally, Chris Townsend's encyclopaedic tome in Cicerone's World Mountain Ranges series, *Scotland,* is also a superb all-round read.

GETTING THERE

If you're travelling to the UK from abroad, you may need to obtain an entry visa. You can check this online with the UK Border Agency at **www.ukvisas.gov.uk**. Glasgow and Edinburgh both have large, international airports. Fort William, the southern end of the trail and the usual starting point, is accessible by train and coach. Trains to Fort William run from Glasgow Queen Street station (most UK mainline rail connections are through Glasgow Central, a short walk away). The train journey from Glasgow is an experience in itself, crossing the bleak Rannoch Moor before arriving into Fort William. The Caledonian Sleeper makes a nightly trip from London to Fort William, with various stops en route. For more details see **www.scotrail.co.uk**. Cape Wrath is generally reached by train from Inverness to Lairg and bus from Lairg to Durness or Kinlochbervie. For more detailed information see 'Access to and return from Cape Wrath' below.

Arkle and Loch Stack (Stage 12)

GETTING AROUND

The remoteness of much of the route means that there are a limited number of points at which you can join or escape. Strathcarron is on the Inverness to Kyle of Lochalsh (Skye) train line: for information about trains see www.scotrail.co.uk. Shiel Bridge, Kinlochewe, Dundonnell, Ullapool, Inchnadamph, Rhiconich, Kinlochbervie and Durness all have bus services. Traveline Scotland (www.travelinescotland.com) is an invaluable resource for planning journeys – it even has a handy journey planner app for smartphones. The Royal Mail also operates a Postbus service in remote areas of the Highlands, where for a small fee you can share a minibus with a friendly postie and a few sacks of mail. It's a fantastic way to travel and the postmen are generally only too willing to share their local knowledge as you bounce along the remote Highland roads. At the time of writing these services are under review: it would be a great shame if they were to disappear. For more information about these services see www.royalmail. com/you-home/your-community/ postbus/routefinder.

Access to and return from Cape Wrath
Cape Wrath itself is inaccessible by direct road. A bus and passenger ferry service runs from the beginning of May every day until the end of September, weather, wind, tides, demand and military operations permitting. It crosses the Kyle of Durness and brings visitors from Keodale (just outside Durness) to the Cape and provides walkers with a handy means of escape without the need to backtrack to Kinlochbervie. The ferry service is operated by John Morrison (01971 511246). The bus service is operated by James Mather (01971 511284, 07742 670 196, james.mather5038@btinternet.com). Details of the services, particularly during MOD exercises, should always be checked in advance. Other useful sources of information are the Tourist Information Centre at Durness (01971 511368) and www.capewrath.org.uk.

In the months of May and September the first ferry leaves Keodale at approximately 1100 each day, including Sundays (the crossing takes about half an hour). There is usually an afternoon sailing leaving Keodale between 1330 and 1400. Throughout June, July and August the first ferry leaves at around 0930 on weekdays and Saturdays, services then run throughout the day on demand. On Sundays throughout the season, the first ferry leaves at 1100, with the last return sailings in the late afternoon. At the time of writing, the adult single fare from the Cape Wrath lighthouse to Keodale was £9.50 inclusive of ferry and minibus (for the latest information see www.capewrathferry.co.uk).

Outside of the main season, there is no real alternative but to retreat to Kinlochbervie. If you are desperate to reach Durness, you can follow the 4x4 track to the ferry crossing (about 11 miles, perhaps using Kearvaig bothy as a stopping point) before heading inland around the Kyle of Durness, but this is very rough ground. A bus service leaves Durness at 0810 (Monday–Saturday), calls in at the Post Office in Kinlochbervie at around 0900 and then goes onwards to meet the Inverness train at Lairg. Check this service locally as the time and location of departures can vary. In summer months, direct coach services to Inverness may be available. For more information about reaching Durness see www.travelinescotland.com and www.capewrathchallenge.co.uk. At the time of writing, the land and buildings at Cape Wrath have been put up for sale by the Northern Lighthouse Board, their current owner. Although the land is subject to a community right to buy notice, the Ministry of Defence has also expressed an interest in acquiring the land. This has caused some concern locally about access to the cape. For the latest information check www.capewrathtrailguide.org.

WHEN TO GO

April, May and June can be ideal months to walk the trail as the days are long, the midges less prevalent and there can be spells of fine weather (although this being Scotland you should go prepared for anything).

Blizzard hits, Glen Oykel (Stage 10)

Benmore Lodge (Stage 10)

September and October are also good, but there may be diversions due to deer stalking and military operations at the cape. In July and August the days are superbly long and the weather can be glorious, but the midges will be in full flight. The limited accommodation along the trail may also be fully booked at this time of year. An attempt outside these months is possible but will require a good deal of skill, experience and expertise in the mountains. You may need specialist equipment (crampons, ice axe) and you're likely to encounter heavy storms, very cold conditions and as little as six hours of daylight, making a daily distance of 20km around the practical limit. Be prepared to abandon your journey and be fully aware of foul weather route alternatives.

ACCOMMODATION

There is generally not a great deal of choice in this part of the world and availability is very much dependent on the time of year. While it's technically possible to walk the route without carrying a tent, using a combination of bothies and other accommodation, it's not prudent to do so. Bothies can occasionally be full to bursting, and you'll lack the flexibility to vary your days if you're feeling tired. Given that some stages are pretty remote, a tent is also an important part of mountain safety should one of your party get injured.

Accommodation listings are usually the first thing to go out of date in any printed guidebook. A current list is offered here as Appendix B, but you should also consult the constantly updated accommodation listings maintained at www.capewrathtrailguide.org/accommodation. In many places along the route accommodation options are very limited, if they exist at all, so it's a good idea to book in advance, especially in summer months. Many of the more remote establishments close during the off season (typically October to March). Accommodation lists can also be obtained from VisitScotland (0845 2255121, www.visitscotland.com). Good, inexpensive accommodation is also available from the Scottish Youth Hostel Association (www.syha.org.uk) or the many independent hostels and bunkhouses (www.hostel-scotland.co.uk).

Bothies and the Mountain Bothy Association

The mission of the Mountain Bothy Association is 'to maintain simple shelters in remote country for the benefit of all who love wild and lonely places.' Even if you are planning to camp or use hotel/hostel accommodation along the trail, it's a good idea to have an awareness of bothy locations in case of emergencies or foul weather. In times gone by, bothy locations were not shared widely and only available with MBA membership. These days the MBA displays bothy locations on its website, however all the charity's maintenance work is carried out by volunteers and it relies on membership to continue its work. A full membership subscription costs around £20 per year, available at www.mountainbothies.org.uk.

Bothies work on a system of trust and respect which breaks down when people don't abide by a few simple rules:

- Leave the bothy clean and tidy with dry kindling for the next visitors
- Make all visitors welcome
- Don't leave graffiti or vandalise the bothy
- Take out all rubbish which you can't burn
- Don't leave perishable food
- Bury human waste well away from the bothy and any water sources
- Make sure the doors and windows are properly closed when you leave.

Not all bothies are operated by the MBA, although their bothies tend to be the best cared for. Some estates also have bothies (for example Glenfinnan), offering varying levels of comfort. Some even have flushing toilets, although this is a rare luxury. Bothies are a unique part of walking in the Scottish Highlands and a rite of passage well worth experiencing. There are few better things than arriving at a remote bothy dripping wet from a howling storm to find a glowing fire ablaze in the hearth and a few fellow mountain lovers with whom to swap far-fetched mountain escapades. That said, bothies can sometimes be cold, rather spooky places if you're on your own or don't have fuel for a fire (most areas around bothies are stripped bare of usable wood) so you may prefer the warm solitude of your tent. Bothies that are on or close to the route or route variants are listed in the relevant route sections, and in Appendix B, with their grid refs.

SAFETY

The Cape Wrath Trail crosses some of the remotest country in Britain, so you must be largely self-sufficient. At times you may be a day or more away from the nearest road, let alone help. For each day plan an escape route in case something goes wrong, or you cannot continue as planned (for example an uncrossable river).

Dangers you may encounter include:

• Sudden weather changes – mists, gales, rain and snow may move in more quickly or be more severe than forecast (always have a refuge and escape route planned)

• Impassable rivers due to heavy rain (have an escape route or the ability to camp and wait for the water levels to subside)

• Ice on the path – a distinct possibility early or late in the year (carry and know how to use an ice-axe and lightweight walking crampons if these conditions are likely)

• Excessive cold or heat (have the clothing and equipment to cope)

• Exhaustion (recognise the signs, rest and keep warm)

Finiskaig River (Stage 3)

- Passage of time (allow plenty of extra time in winter, in poor weather and over rough terrain).

River crossings

River crossings are one of the greatest hazards on this route. In normal conditions, most mountain streams and rivers in Scotland are wide and shallow, with pebbly bottoms, making them relatively safe and easy to wade across where there are no bridges (a common occurrence given the remoteness of much of the trail). But a small burn that can be easily crossed in dry weather can quickly turn into a dangerous torrent after sustained rain. Crossing rivers and streams at the wrong time, in the wrong place can and does kill people and this unpredictability makes it impossible to provide warnings for all crossings. The route has been designed to avoid crossings that are known to be dangerous in very wet conditions. Potentially tricky crossings are noted but you should assume that all river crossings in wet weather will be more difficult and factor this into your timing and route planning.

After a long day in rough country, particularly if you're behind schedule, the temptation can be to 'plough through' a river. But if you're unsure about the safety of any crossing, a detour upstream will generally turn up either a safer crossing point or a bridge that isn't marked on the map.

River Oykel, near its source (Stage 10)

If in doubt, find somewhere else to cross or do not cross at all, as rivers subside quickly when the rain stops. With common sense and by familiarising yourself with some basic river crossing techniques, you should be able to deal with anything you encounter on this trail. Consider using walking pole(s) to provide additional stability when crossing. The British Mountaineering Council (BMC) provides an excellent guide to river crossings as part of their Hill Skills series: www.thebmc.co.uk/hillskills.

Given the number of river crossings, it's also worth giving some prior thought to how you'll deal with wet feet. This can be a real problem, with blistering from damp footwear being one of the main reasons people have to abandon the trail. Some choose to strip off their socks and cross in boots alone. This approach seems to hold limited advantage as sodden boots soon lead to sodden socks. Others carry a lightweight pair of plastic sandals that can be worn for river crossings, thus keeping boots and socks dry.

Personally I find the process of trying to keep your boots and socks dry time consuming and fairly fruitless given the sheer amount of bog and water to be crossed. My favoured approach is to use Gore-Tex socks and a good gaiter. Whilst these won't keep you completely dry, they prevent the worst of the water getting at your feet and greatly reduce the amount of time spent faffing about at the edge of burns.

Pests

In general the flora and fauna in this part of the world are unlikely to cause you any harm, but there are a few things you need to look out for.

Ticks

The incidence of Lyme Disease caused by a bite from a tick, a small parasite, has been on the increase in Scotland. It is a serious and potentially fatal disease. Ticks are common in woodland, heathland and areas of Scotland where deer graze. Insect repellent and long trousers are the best prevention and you should check yourself regularly. Ticks can be removed by gripping them close to the skin with tweezers and pulling backwards without jerking or twisting. Don't try to burn them off. Symptoms of Lyme Disease vary but can include a rash and flu-like symptoms that are hard to diagnose. Most cases of Lyme Disease can be cured with antibiotics, especially if treated early in the course of illness. The Mountaineering Council of Scotland has a useful tick advice video on its website: www.mcofs.org.uk.

Midges

Midges are a voracious scourge of the western Highlands, at their peak between the end of May and early October. There are more than 40 species of biting midge in Scotland, but luckily only five of these regularly feed on people. Even so, their bite causes itching and swelling that can

River Dessarry (Stage 3)

last several days. Unless you've experienced the sensation of being 'eaten alive' by a cloud of Scottish midges, it's hard to understand just how unpleasant they can be. In summer, they can generally be relied upon to spoil beautiful lochside sunsets. Unfortunately the Cape Wrath Trail passes through through the very heart of midge country. The only real prevention is insect repellent or physical barriers such as head nets. From experience DEET based repellent products work most effectively, although they have an unpleasant aroma of chemicals and should be kept away from plastics and sensitive fabrics like Gore-Tex. Citronella candles also

work well and many people swear by Avon Skin So Soft (available from www.avon.uk.com).

Some people maintain that light-coloured clothing also keeps midges at bay, although I haven't personally noted a particular preference for the high fashion hues of modern outdoor gear. Unfortunately even when repellents are used without a physical barrier such as a net, midges will still land and crawl on you. The good news is that midges can't fly in even the gentlest of breezes, which are not usually in short supply in this part of the world and they dislike strong sunlight (should you see any). Such is the impact of the Scottish midge that it now has its own forecast and Apple iPhone app. For more information see www.midgeforecast.co.uk.

Weather

The northwestern Highlands of Scotland is one of the wettest places in Europe, with annual rainfall of up to 4,500mm (180 inches) falling on as many as 265 days a year. Due to the mountainous terrain, warm, wet air is forced to rise on contact with the coast, where it cools and condenses, forming clouds. Atlantic depressions bring wind and clouds regularly throughout the year and are a common feature in the autumn and winter. Like the rest of the United Kingdom, prevailing wind from the southwest brings around 30 days of severe gales each year. The combined effect of wind and rain can make walking hazardous at times, even in relatively low-lying areas, so you should always have an escape plan.

EMERGENCIES

In an emergency, dial 999, ask for the police, then state that you need mountain rescue. Be ready to give a detailed situation report – the mnemonic 'CHALET' may help you remember vital information under pressure:

- **C**asualties – number, names (and, if known, age), type of injuries (for example lower leg, head injury, collapse, drowning)
- **H**azards to the rescuers – for example, strong winds, rock fall

- **A**ccess – the name of mountain area and description of the terrain. It may also be appropriate to describe the approach and any distinguishing features of your location (for example an orange survival bag). Information on the weather conditions at the incident site is also useful, particularly if you are in cloud or mist
- **L**ocation of the incident – a grid reference and a description. Don't forget to give the map sheet number and state if the grid reference is from a GPS device
- **E**quipment at the scene – for example, torches, other mobile phones (including their numbers), group shelters, medical personnel
- **T**ype of incident – a brief description of the time and apparent cause of the incident.

If you are unable to telephone for help, use a whistle and repeat a series of six long blasts, separated by a gap of one minute. Carry on the whistle blasts until someone reaches you and don't stop because you've heard a reply, as rescuers may be using your blasts to help locate you. At night use a torch to signal in the same pattern.

A service now enables texts to be sent to the emergency number 999 when voice calls cannot be made, but where there is sufficient signal to send a text. To use the service you'll need to pre-register via a text – send 'register' to 999 and you'll get a reply with further instructions. If using the service in an emergency, you should wait until you receive a reply from the emergency services before assuming help has been summoned. Further details, including guidelines on how to register, can be found at www.emergencysms.org.uk.

MONEY AND COMMUNICATIONS

It's a good idea to carry a supply of cash with you as cards are not universally accepted and cash-points are few and far between. Cashpoints can be found in Fort William, Kinlochewe, Ullapool and Kinlochbervie (located in the Spar supermarket at the harbour).

Post Offices can be found in the larger towns (Fort William, Kinlochewe, Ullapool and Kinlochbervie) and most small villages have post boxes. Post Offices may also hold parcels for collection (they need to be addressed to the Post Office itself and marked 'Post Restante' and you'll need photo identification to collect: see www.postoffice.co.uk for more details). Most hotels and hostels will also hold parcels for residents if you ask them in advance.

Mobile phone coverage is distinctly patchy in the northwest Highlands and shouldn't be relied upon. If you're worried about mobile phone coverage, 'pay-as-you-go' SIM cards for the main UK networks can be bought cheaply and used in 'unlocked' mobile phones to ensure you can connect to any available network. Internet data access via mobile phone is rarely possible outside larger areas of civilisation and even then it's likely to be a slow GPRS connection rather than 3G. An increasing number of hotels offer internet access via wi-fi.

English is spoken throughout the Scottish Highlands, although the broad local brogue can sometimes take a bit of getting used to if English is not your first language. You may also encounter some Gaelic, a beautiful but rarely spoken language.

PREPARATION AND PLANNING

It is with some justification that the Cape Wrath Trail is regarded as the toughest long distance backpacking trail in Britain. Dotted here and there, you may come across signs that guard the entry to particularly remote sections: 'Take Care – You are entering remote, sparsely populated, potentially dangerous mountain country – Please ensure that you are adequately experienced and equipped to complete your journey without assistance'.

It is hard to improve on this pithy warning – this is rough, unforgiving country that should not be underestimated. There are no pack carrying services and often there are not even any clear paths, only bogs and leg-sapping terrain. Limited re-supply points require self-sufficiency for much of the journey, and there will be stretches during which you'll need

Stand of pines, Glendessarry (Stage 3)

to carry many days' supplies. **This is absolutely not a route for beginners or those unfamiliar with remote, rugged mountain areas.** It is in a totally different league to other Highland trails like the West Highland Way, where civilisation is never far away.

The journey usually takes two to three weeks and the cumulative effect of sustained daily exertion is substantial. Don't be afraid to start with a few shorter days and build rest stops into your schedule. To borrow from the lexicon of football managers, this is a marathon, not a sprint. With a decent level of overall fitness and mountain experience you should be able safely to enjoy your weeks on the trail.

WHAT TO TAKE

The choice of equipment for any expedition is intensely personal. On such a long and arduous trip, there is a temptation to err on the side of lighter weight, but given the likelihood of harsh weather at any time of year, you'll need to strike a sensible balance between weight and function. The list below is not designed to be comprehensive, but offers a broad outline of the kind of equipment you'll need to be considering. For more information about expedition kit see www.capewrathtrailguide.org.

Camping and carrying
- Rucksack (a large expedition sack, well used in advance to ensure that it is properly broken in for the trail)
- Tent (suitable for four season mountain use)
- Sleeping bag (suitably rated for the time of year and able to cope with damp conditions)
- Sleeping mat

Kitchen
- Stove
- Fuel (with sufficient spare to allow for emergencies)
- Pots/pans
- Water container
- Knife, fork, spoon

Footwear
- Strong mountain boots
- Sandals for bothy, tent
- Gaiters

Clothing
- Waterproof shell jacket (ideally 3 layer membrane, eg Event, Gore Tex Pro Shell or Paramo)
- Waterproof trousers
- Walking trousers, shorts (for the optimist)
- Base layer (top and long johns)
- Midlayer (eg fleece, softshell)
- Insulating layer (eg down or primaloft jacket/gilet)
- Socks and spares
- Waterproof socks
- Hat
- Balaclava/neck gaiter (spring, autumn)
- Gloves/mitts with spares

Accessories
- Walking pole(s) (highly recommended given the roughness of terrain and frequent river crossings)
- Survival bag/blanket
- Whistle
- Torch and spare batteries
- Stuffsacs, drysacs
- Waterproof document wallet
- Compass
- Maps
- Guidebook
- Notebook, pens
- First aid kit
- Mobile phone
- Toilet trowel
- Wash kit
- Camera
- GPS, spare batteries

Food and drink
The remoteness of large stretches of the Cape Wrath Trail make a large degree of self-sufficiency essential. There are some shops along the way where supplies can be purchased, but even these are small and often limited in what they can offer (listed in Appendix C). In mountain areas it is generally fine to drink water directly from the streams, but in areas where there are livestock, or lower down the glens, the water should be sterilised before drinking.

The Cape Wrath Trail is not an official route and is not currently waymarked at any point. If you're intending on wild camping during your journey to the cape there are a few simple rules you need to be aware of. The Land Reform (Scotland) Act 2003 gives statutory access to Scotland's outdoors, extending from the parks and open spaces in towns to the remote and wild areas of land and water in the Highlands. This is sometimes referred to as the 'right to roam'.

The Scottish Outdoor Access Code is based on three main principles that are actually pretty good codes for life in general:

• respect for the interests of other people
• care for the environment
• responsibility for one's own actions.

Access rights include wild camping, as long as this is lightweight and done by small numbers. You can wild camp wherever access rights apply, but avoid camping in enclosed fields of crops or near farm animals and keep well away from buildings, roads and historic structures. Take extra care to avoid disturbing deer stalking or grouse shooting. If you wish to camp close to a house or building, ask for the owner's permission. Leave no trace and take away all litter. Guidance about how best to enjoy wild camping is available from the Mountaineering Council of Scotland website: www.mcofs.org.uk/assets/pdfs/wildcamping.pdf. For more information on access in Scotland see www.outdooraccess-scotland.com.

Deer stalking

Deer stalking is an important part of the sustainable management of deer populations in upland habitats, where deer are culled humanely each year. The red stag stalking season is from 1 July to 20 October, although the dates that individual estates start stalking vary. September and October are particularly busy months, when stalking is often taking place six days a week. Hinds (female deer) are culled from 21 October to 15 February, with most activity taking place before Christmas.

Roe stalking can also take place on forested estates. The roe buck stalking season is from 1 April to 20 October, with June to August being the most important months, and the doe stalking season is from 21 October to 31 March. Deer stalking does not usually take place on Sundays.

In upland areas of Scotland many estates have used hill phones to provide a recorded message giving information about local stalking activity. At the time of writing, these hill phones are being phased out and replaced with a web service called Heading for the Scottish Hills which can be found at www.outdooraccess-scotland.com. The Mountaineering Council of Scotland also provides advice via its website: www.mcofs.org.uk/hillphones.asp.

Sign, Attadale Forest (Stage 5)

MAPS AND NAVIGATION

Choice of maps is quite a personal thing. Some prefer the extra detail of the Ordnance Survey 1:25,000 scale on mountainous sections, others like to have maps of this scale available at all times. Some swear by Harvey maps, others find them difficult to interpret. Carrying paper maps will add a fair bit of weight to your pack so it's worth giving some thought to the different options.

If you opt to carry the original paper maps, you can post them home from points of civilisation with pre-paid envelopes once they have served their purpose. The advantage is that you'll have the full maps available at all times, but you'll have to put up with extra weight. A map case is

essential to keep your maps in good repair as a bit of 'scotch mist' (a local euphemism for torrential rain) can reduce an unprotected map to mulch in a matter of minutes. Laminated versions of Ordnance Survey maps (called ActiveMaps) are available for many OS sheets, although they are heavier and more expensive than the regular versions. All Harvey maps are both waterproof and lightweight, but they do not currently cover the full trail.

There is an increasingly wide range of Ordnance Survey mapping programmes for personal computers that allow you to plan and print the relevant sections of the route: MemoryMap, Quo and Anquet are the market leaders. There are also a number of good web-based route planners that allow you to plot your journey – Grough, Trailzilla and Walk Highlands all work well, with slightly different features. Toughprint paper can be used to print weatherproof maps at home or you could make colour photocopies from your OS maps which can then be laminated. Although this approach will save weight, you may find yourself lacking the wider map area and context needed in an emergency or for a detour. Weight savings must always be balanced with safety.

A full list of Ordnance Survey and Harvey maps covering the Cape Wrath Trail can be found in Appendix E. To walk the trail safely you will need to be a competent navigator, confident in taking, setting and walking on bearings and orientating yourself in low visibility on featureless terrain. If you are carrying a GPS device

it should only be used as an aid, not as your primary method of navigation. No electronic device can be completely relied upon in the outdoors environment, particularly one as wet as Scotland.

USING THIS GUIDE

The guide is split into three main sections: Fort William to Strathcarron, Strathcarron to Inverlael (near Ullapool) and Inverlael to Cape Wrath. All of the points above allow reasonable access by bus or train if you want to pick up or leave the trail. The guide is written south to north, Fort William to Cape Wrath, but the walk is equally rewarding walked in the opposite direction, although lacking such an impressive finale. The sections themselves are sub-divided into a series of stages. These stages are not intended

Climbing through Drochaid Coire Lair (Alternative Stage 6)

to exactly correspond with single days of walking, although in some cases they do. Varying age, ability and terrain make it difficult and potentially dangerous to suggest generic mountain days to follow rigidly. Some stages can be walked comfortably in a day, others may be possible in a day but require a long, hard slog and some may require two or even three days. The aim of this guide is to allow you to create a personal itinerary, based on your own pace, needs and ability.

The main route deliberately steers near what few hotels, hostels or bothies there are in this part of the world, where it is practical and not too circuitous to do so. Although it is in theory possible to walk the trail without a tent, you'll find this severely limits your options and from a mountain safety point of view, carrying some sort of shelter on the remoter sections is definitely advisable, if not essential. To help you plan your route, each stage notes accommodation and some wild camping options as well as any amenities and transport options available. Detailed route descriptions and corresponding OS maps are provided for each stage. Although every effort has been made to ensure accuracy, things change on the ground. Paths fall into disuse, new ones spring up and bridges come and go. You can keep up-to-date with changes at www.capewrathtrailguide.org.

To prepare you for the ground ahead the route descriptions generally state the type of tracks you'll be following. Broadly speaking these fall into four main categories: 'good' (visible, continuous and easy to follow over relatively easy terrain), 'rough' (visible, continuous and fairly easy to follow, but ground may be boggy and/or rocky), '4x4 track' (generally double width, often with some sort of surface) and 'indistinct' (not well defined, may disappear or be hard to follow at certain sections, generally over rough terrain).

One of the great attractions of the Cape Wrath Trail is the number of alternatives to the main route that are possible. This sets it apart from other tightly waymarked trails, and gives you much greater choice. This guide has tried to strike a balance between choice and complexity. The alternatives described within each section are mainly the most obvious or well-established. Other possible alternatives are noted in each stage of the main route description. These range from shorter options on easier terrain to more technical routes for those either seeking an even greater challenge, or who are allergic to civilisation.

There will be those that regard any attempt to codify this route as something approaching sacrilege, but this guide tries to strike the right balance between providing useful and necessary information to support the planning of a trip without an overly prescriptive approach. Make it what you will and go where the glens and weather take you.

1 FORT WILLIAM TO STRATHCARRON
109km, 5–7 days

Overlooking Loch Hourn (Stage 4)

1 FORT WILLIAM TO STRATHCARRON

Loch Linnhe, Fort William

The Cape Wrath Trail is not a route that eases you in gently. You'll quickly find yourself deep in some of the remotest and roughest areas of Scotland. The terrain and the time it can take to cover relatively short distances often catches people out, so take this first section steadily. The stage to Glenfinnan is fairly forgiving, but as you leave Glendessarry it's pretty unrelenting all the way to Strathcarron. For all its difficulty, this is arguably the most stunning section of the trail. Each stage has its own unique challenges and rewards, from the rugged beauty of Knoydart to the showy spectacle of the Falls of Glomach. By the time you reach Strathcarron your feet will be sore but you'll already have plenty of stories to tell.

STAGE 1
Fort William to Glenfinnan

Start	Fort William
Finish	Glenfinnan Monument
Distance	34.3km (21¼ miles)
Ascent	610m
Average duration	1–2 days
Terrain	Mostly easy walking along road, 4x4 tracks and clear paths
Maps	OS Landranger 41 (Ben Nevis); 40 (Mallaig & Glenfinnan): OS Explorer 391 (Ardgour & Strontian)
Amenities	Hotels, bunkhouse (Glenfinnan); Corryhully bothy (NM 912 844)
Camping	Good riverside camping spots in Cona Glen and Glenfinnan

The start of any great adventure needs a sense of theatre and the ferry from Fort William to Camusnagaul provides it. As you head towards the hills of the Ardgour peninsula and alight at the pier at Camusnagaul you've already made a firm step away from civilisation. Despite being so close to Fort William, the Ardgour peninsula feels immediately remote and cut off, and you can't help but feel slightly nervous as you strike off on the first steps of this epic journey. Counterintuitively you start your journey to the most northwesterly point of Scotland by heading almost due south.

The main route follows the road south along the shores of Loch Linnhe before turning inland up Cona Glen. At just over 20 miles, this is a long first day if tackled in one go, so you may choose to ease yourself into the walk and camp short of Glenfinnan. There is an estate bothy in the glen that is generally locked but there are good camping spots by the river. From Cona Glen the path turns north and climbs over the shoulder of Meall na Cuartaige before descending to the Glenfinnan Monument that guards the northern end of the serpentine Loch Shiel.

Looking across Loch Linnhe from Fort William

Map continues on page 41

Every couple of hours from Monday to Saturday the rusty boat slips out from Fort William's **pier** onto the dark waters of Loch Linnhe, leaving behind the cars bustling along the loch-side road.

38

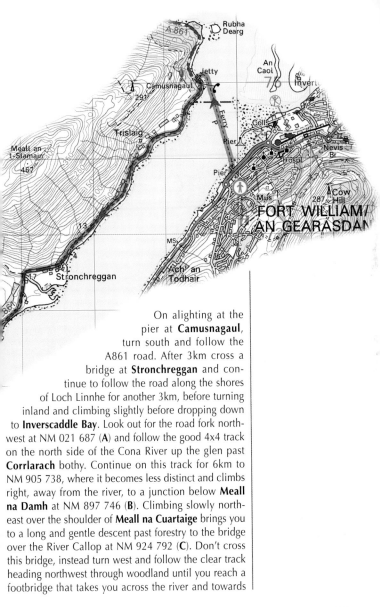

On alighting at the pier at **Camusnagaul**, turn south and follow the A861 road. After 3km cross a bridge at **Stronchreggan** and continue to follow the road along the shores of Loch Linnhe for another 3km, before turning inland and climbing slightly before dropping down to **Inverscaddle Bay**. Look out for the road fork northwest at NM 021 687 (**A**) and follow the good 4x4 track on the north side of the Cona River up the glen past **Corrlarach** bothy. Continue on this track for 6km to NM 905 738, where it becomes less distinct and climbs right, away from the river, to a junction below **Meall na Damh** at NM 897 746 (**B**). Climbing slowly northeast over the shoulder of **Meall na Cuartaige** brings you to a long and gentle descent past forestry to the bridge over the River Callop at NM 924 792 (**C**). Don't cross this bridge, instead turn west and follow the clear track heading northwest through woodland until you reach a footbridge that takes you across the river and towards the **Glenfinnan Monument**. Glenfinnan's railway station and hotels lie about a kilometre west from here along the road.

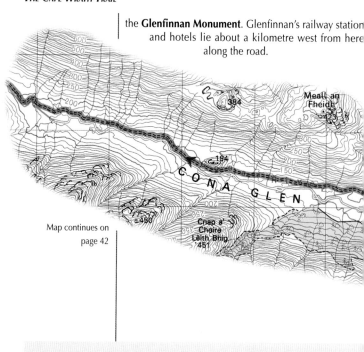

Map continues on page 42

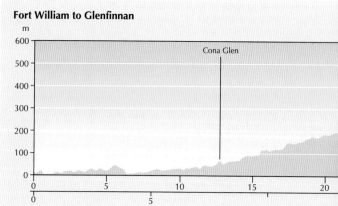

Fort William to Glenfinnan

Glenfinnan itself has a couple of smart hotels and a bunkhouse at the train station. Further up the glen is a well kept estate bothy at Corryhully. Even further up the glen good camping spots abound by the River Finnan, giving you a head start on the next day's journey.

Route alternatives

From Camusnagaul you could choose instead to follow the A861 road north and east around the shores of Loch Eil. ▶ But it seems a shame to skirt the rugged inner

This is probably the quietest A road you'll encounter.

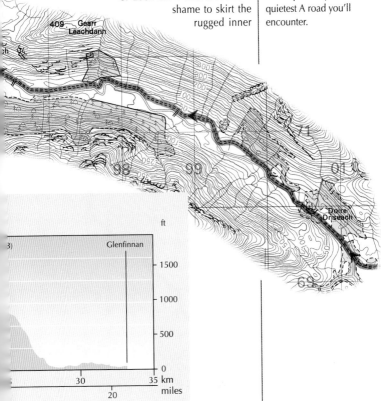

beauty of the peninsula and it brings you out some way from the amenities at Glenfinnan.

A major alternative start to the Cape Wrath Trail has been suggested by Cameron McNeish that initially follows the Great Glen Way. It's a slightly easier start to the walk and gives access to more easterly country than the main route, which may appeal to some. From Fort William you follow the Great Glen Way along Loch Lochy and pass by Invergarry into the beautiful Glen Garry, before traversing the spectacular Glen Loyne to Cluanie. The route then heads north towards the hostel at Alltbeithe. From here you have a couple of choices to rejoin the main route. You could head west along Fionngleann and Gleann Lichd to Morvich, rejoining this guide's main route at Stage 5, or take the spectacularly wild route northwest along Gleann Gnìomhaidh, turning north along Gleann Gaorsaic to Carnach. Either is superb – this is wonderful country. ▶

This route is described in Alternative Stages 1 to 3

STAGE 2
Glenfinnan to Glen Dessarry

Start	Glenfinnan Monument
Finish	A'Chùil bothy (NM 944 924)
Distance	18.1km (11¼ miles)
Ascent	600m
Average Duration	1 day
Terrain	4x4 tracks in Glenfinnan and Glen Dessarry with some rough country in between on mainly well defined paths
Maps	OS Landranger 40 (Mallaig & Glenfinnan): OS Explorer 398 (Loch Morar & Mallaig)
Amenities	Corryhully Bothy (NM 912 844) A'Chùil bothy (NM 944 924)

Glenfinnan itself is stunningly beautiful although it has been rather spoilt by a recent hydro-electric development; one can only hope the wounds heal quickly. The route starts at Glenfinnan's monument, soon passing under the railway viaduct. The estate bothy at Corryhully is a good stopping spot before the track becomes steadily rougher and climbs up and over the bealach watched over by the twin sentinels of Streap and Sgùrr Thuilm.

The ascent is slow and steady but the subsequent descent is initially steep and rough. As you descend Gleann Cuìrnean, the path becomes steadily rougher. The bothy at A'Chùil makes an ideal overnight stop but there are also some good camping spots further up the glen along the River Dessarry. If you are fit and strong you could push on towards Sourlies but that makes it a long hard day so early in the journey.

From the **monument** ascend to the main road and follow it northwest for about half a kilometre, crossing a bridge over the River Finnan before turning immediately north at NM 906 808 to pass under the **viaduct**.

Before you leave Glenfinnan, as you pass under the arc of its **viaduct**, it's worth taking a moment to savour this wonderful location. The viaduct and monument guard the head of the loch and for once human endeavour and the wild landscape seem strangely at peace.

The viaduct has been made famous of late by its appearances in the Harry Potter films. Built by Sir Robert McAlpine between 1897 and 1901, it forms part of

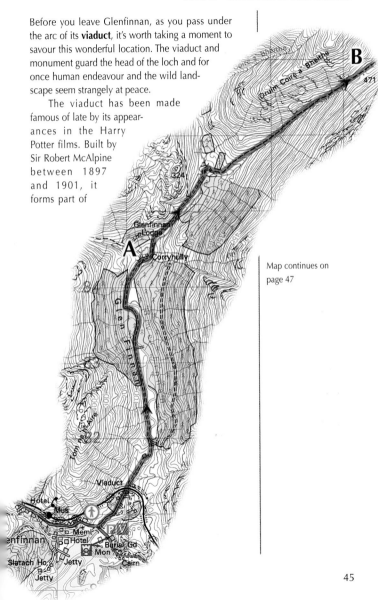

Map continues on page 47

Bealach below Streap, Glen Finnan

the Mallaig extension of the West Highland Line. Connecting Fort William and Mallaig, the line was a crucial artery for the local fishing industry and the Highlands economy and is considered to be one of the most picturesque train journeys in the world.

Passing beneath the viaduct marks your first steps onto the trail proper towards the rough bounds of Knoydart.

The path is distinct most of the way, but some of the burn crossings may be tricky in spate.

◀ The paved road takes you up **Glen Finnan** on the west side of the river all the way to **Corryhully** bothy (**A**). Bear right and pass the bothy, following a 4x4 track on the west side of the river up to the bridge at NM 921 856. From the bridge, a clear track climbs steadily up to the pass between **Streap** and **Sgùrr Thuilm** (**B**) (spot height of 471m on the OS map), zig-zagging across the burn at various points. ◀ Crossing the bealach through an old line of iron fence posts brings you to a steep descent into **Gleann Cuìrnean**. The first kilometre is distinctly tricky, particularly in wet or icy conditions: care should be taken, particularly with a heavy rucksack. Once you reach the base of the slope, follow the clear path to the west of the river: it disappears in places due to bank erosion.

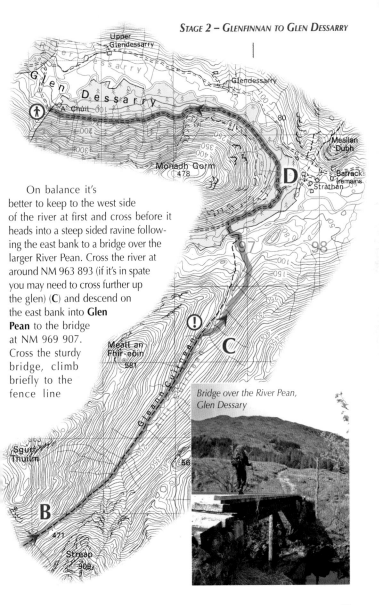

On balance it's better to keep to the west side of the river at first and cross before it heads into a steep sided ravine following the east bank to a bridge over the larger River Pean. Cross the river at around NM 963 893 (if it's in spate you may need to cross further up the glen) (**C**) and descend on the east bank into **Glen Pean** to the bridge at NM 969 907. Cross the sturdy bridge, climb briefly to the fence line

Bridge over the River Pean, Glen Dessary

47

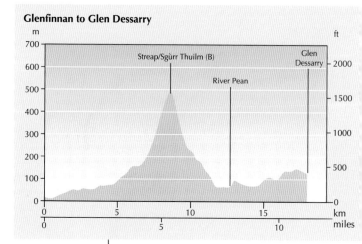

Glenfinnan to Glen Dessarry

and walk 100m to the west to pick up a boggy path that leads north into the woods, climbing to meet a 4x4 track. Follow this track east (right) for about a kilometre before turning left at a fork (**D**) and taking the track onwards into **Glen Dessarry**, towards **A'Chùil** bothy (NM 944 924).

Route alternatives

An alternative route heads north from Drumsallie at the head of Loch Eil north up Gleann Fionn Lighe, climbing to the bealach of Gualann nan Osna before traversing Gleann Camgharaidh and descending to join the main route at the bridge in Glen Pean. This alternative is only really worth considering if you chose to head north from Camusnagaul via the Loch Eil side alternative to the first stage.

STAGE 3
Glen Dessarry to Barisdale

Start	A'Chùil bothy (NM 944 924)
Finish	Barisdale
Distance	24.8km (15½ miles)
Ascent	930m
Average duration	1–2 days
Terrain	Tough walking on mainly rough, boggy paths. Steep climb to Mam Unndalain
Maps	OS Landranger 40 (Mallaig & Glenfinnan); 33 (Loch Alsh & Glen Shiel): OS Explorer 398 (Loch Morar & Mallaig); 413 (Knoydart, Loch Hourn & Loch Duich: Harvey British Mountain Map Knoydart, Kintail and Glen Affric
Amenities	Sourlies bothy (NM 869 951); Barisdale Estate (campsite, bothy, self-catering)
Camping	Beside river in Glendessarry, at Sourlies, alongside the River Carnach, bealach at Mam Unndalain

It is with some justification that the area you are entering is known as the rough bounds of Knoydart. The terrain was used extensively for commando training in the Second World War, recognised by the Commando Memorial at Spean Bridge. Loch Arkaig is also reputedly the hiding place of a consignment of gold landed by the French at Arisaig for the Jacobites in 1746 but never found. The going is sufficiently rough to make a short day and an overnight stop at Sourlies worth considering. Set at the foot of Loch Nevis, Sourlies is a wonderfully remote spot and regarded as one of the best located bothies in the country (there's also idyllic camping here by the loch). If you push on to Barisdale it will be a long, tough day even for strong walkers. If you tire there are good camping options by the River Carnach or further up the glen near the ruin at NM 883 993 or slightly further on at NM 890 995.

The walk alongside the River Carnach affords imposing views of Luinne Bheinn to the north before you ascend steeply on very rough ground to a good path that takes you over the bealach and down to Barisdale and Loch Hourn. Barisdale is a small collection of buildings huddled on the southern shores of Loch Hourn enjoying a wide vista that spreads out towards Skye.

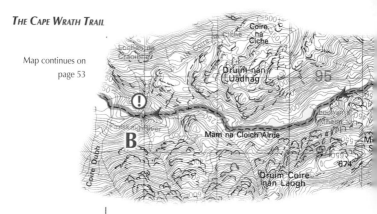

Map continues on
page 53

From A'Chùil bothy follow the 4x4 track which continues along the south side of the river to a bridge at NM 930 934 (**A**). The main path continues along the north bank of the river up through the forest but can be very boggy. If wet, a better option may be to head north from the bridge until you clear the woods, joining the track that comes from upper Glen Dessarry at Allt Coire nan Uth.

Redundant gate and stile, upper Glen Dessarry

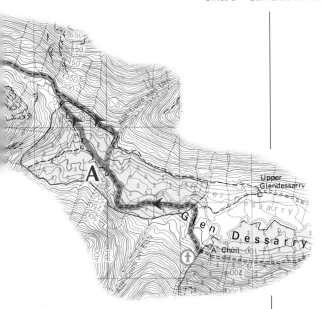

From the end of the forestry, the path to upper Glen Dessarry is initially clear but gets increasingly rough and indistinct as you climb towards **Lochan a Mhaim**. As you pass the lochans, the going improves slightly and the path becomes less rough and more distinct, taking you west to cross the Finiskaig River around NM 890 945 (**B**). ▶

Take care here when the river is in spate.

You'll start to **feel the remoteness** in earnest as you leave Glen Dessarry in the shadow of a trio of giant munros (Sgurr na Ciche, Garbh Chioch Mhor and Sgurr nan Coireachan) and descending along the Finiskaig River the landscape becomes increasingly Tolkeinesque.

Once the river has been successfully crossed, the path climbs briefly before winding steeply down over rocks that can be slippery in wet conditions.

Glen Dessarry to Barisdale

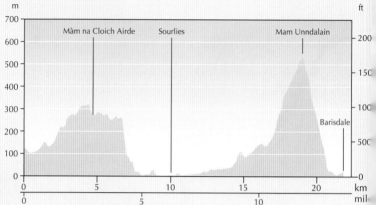

Descending towards Loch Nevis

The **first sight of Loch Nevis** is spectacular: one of Scotland's finest sea lochs, it runs 20km inland from the open sea at the Sound of Sleat. If you're lucky and the tide is out, you'll be able to walk around the headland on the beach.

Crossing another bridge, the path descends to the shores of the loch becoming boggy and taking you directly to **Sourlies** bothy. At low tide it's possible to pass the bothy and skirt the headland along the edge of Loch Nevis. At high tide you'll need to clamber over the promontory behind the bothy, but there's no real path here.

Once you've rounded the headland, head north across the marsh flats to a rickety bridge at **Carnoch** (**C**). There's no clear path here and the ground is very boggy.

Map continues on page 54

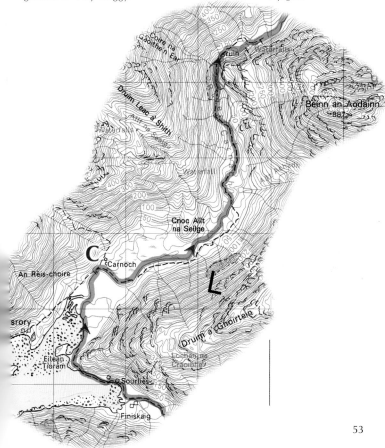

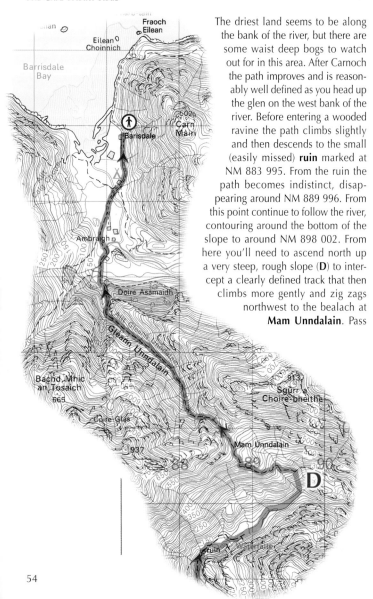

The driest land seems to be along the bank of the river, but there are some waist deep bogs to watch out for in this area. After Carnoch the path improves and is reasonably well defined as you head up the glen on the west bank of the river. Before entering a wooded ravine the path climbs slightly and then descends to the small (easily missed) **ruin** marked at NM 883 995. From the ruin the path becomes indistinct, disappearing around NM 889 996. From this point continue to follow the river, contouring around the bottom of the slope to around NM 898 002. From here you'll need to ascend north up a very steep, rough slope (**D**) to intercept a clearly defined track that then climbs more gently and zig zags northwest to the bealach at **Mam Unndalain**. Pass

River Carnach

through the bealach and descend on a clearly defined track to the north of the river into **Gleann Unndalain** and past the buildings at Ambraigh into **Barisdale**. ▶

There are sweeping views of Beinn Sgritheall towering above Arnisdale to the north and the imposing bulk of Ladhar Bheinn to the west.

There is a campsite and bothy owned by the estate for which there is a small charge. The estate also rents out two larger buildings as accommodation (one sleeping 3–5 people, one 8–12).

Route alternatives
You could head for Inverie by climbing up from Carnoch (a long, steep, drag) and then descending via Gleann Meadail. However, this is quite a detour and you're only just getting off the beaten track. If you did choose this route alternative, you can rejoin the trail by heading north from Inverie up Gleann an Dubh-Lochain to Barisdale.

STAGE 4
Barisdale to Morvich (near Shiel Bridge)

Start	Barisdale
Finish	Morvich
Distance	31.5km (19½ miles)
Ascent	1310m
Average duration	2 days
Terrain	Clear path to Kinloch Hourn and onwards until Allt Coire Mhàlagain. From there rough, mainly trackless ground with a steep, rough climb to Bealach Coire Mhalagain
Maps	OS Landranger 33 (Loch Alsh, Glen Shiel & Loch Hourn): OS Explorer 413 (Knoydart, Loch Hourn & Loch Duich); 414 (Glen Shiel & Kintail Forest); Harvey Superwalker Kintail (Glen Shiel)
Amenities	Kinloch Hourn Farm (café, B&B); campsites (Shiel Bridge, Morvich); Youth Hostel (Ratagan); hotel and B&B (Shiel Bridge). Shiel Bridge petrol station sells a limited range of food and supplies
Camping	Various small bays between Barisdale and Kinloch Hourn; small area by bridge in Kinloch Hourn; some flat spots in Allt a Choire Reidh and Allt Coire Mhàlagain; upper Allt a Choire Chaoli; some riverside spots by Allt Undalain

The route onwards from Barisdale looks fairly straightforward on the map, but as so often with this trail the reality is different on the ground. The lochside path to Kinloch Hourn (3–4 hours from Barisdale) is fairly rough, with plenty of short, sharp climbs and descents.

From Kinloch Hourn the trail gains its first serious height and ventures into rough, trackless country as it climbs through the Kinlochhourn forest. After a crossing of Allt a Choire Reidh (which can be very difficult when the river is in spate) the path peters out as you skirt Sgurr na Sgine before a steep, rough climb to Bealach Coire Mhàlagain in the shadows of the impressive Forcan Ridge. The descent to Shiel Bridge is just as taxing with rough boggy ground most of the way. Hence, despite the modest distance, it is generally best spread over two days.

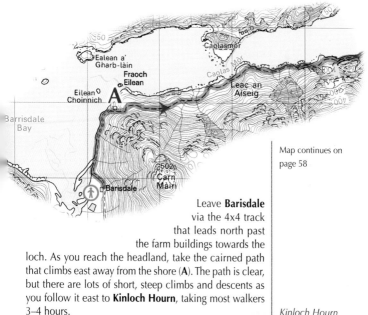

Map continues on
page 58

Leave **Barisdale**
via the 4x4 track
that leads north past
the farm buildings towards the
loch. As you reach the headland, take the cairned path
that climbs east away from the shore (**A**). The path is clear,
but there are lots of short, steep climbs and descents as
you follow it east to **Kinloch Hourn**, taking most walkers
3–4 hours.

Kinloch Hourn

By the time you reach Kinloch Hourn you'll feel like you've done a good day's walk already. There is accommodation and a tea room serving breakfasts, lunches and dinners at Kinloch Hourn Farm (open April to September – book in advance for the accommodation) and camping is possible just over the bridge.

At Kinloch Hourn the track hits a tarmac road, which you follow for 1.5km past the farm, turning left to cross the bridge at NG 953 064 (**B**). Having crossed the bridge, follow the track towards buildings, passing through a white gate. Pass the stalker's cottage on your right and just before you reach the next building, bear right and climb through the pine woods to meet a larger track that climbs northwest beneath large electricity pylons. The path climbs to a pass and affords superb views of Loch Hourn. From the pass descend to a junction at NG 939 081 and take the right hand fork on a clear path that climbs gently to a wooden estate shelter by the river (**C**).

In poor weather conditions you'll need to keep an eye on your navigation here, but in good conditions the **views southwest over Loch Hourn** back towards Barisdale are superb.

A clear path crosses **Allt a Choire Reidh**, steering near the small wooden stalker's hut. The river here will be very difficult to cross in spate, so you may need to try further down where it becomes wider and shallower.

Cross the river with care and follow a clear path that skirts **Sgurr na Signe** into the glen of **Allt Coire Mhàlagain**.

Before long the path disappears and the floor of the glen is rough, so it's best to contour round the lower slopes, keeping to the east side of the glen. The glen eventually narrows, leaving a steep ascent to the bealach. It's best to climb at first on the east side of the river and cross where you can. In the **Bealach Coire Mhàlagain** there is a small lochan which is handy for

Map continues on
page 60

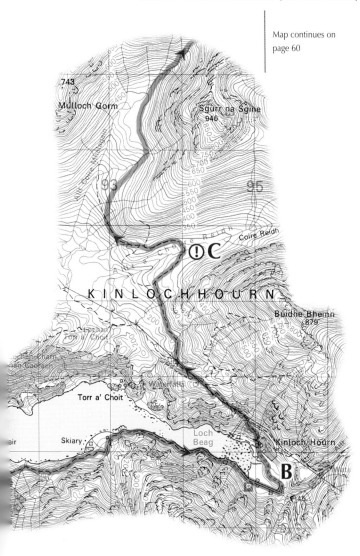

orientation (**D**). Keep to the north side of the lochan and contour northeast to a line of large stones starting about 200m from the lochan. The stones provide a useful handrail and are accompanied by a path of sorts that descends over **Meallan Odhar** before dropping down on a

Map continues on page 62

Barisdale to Morvich

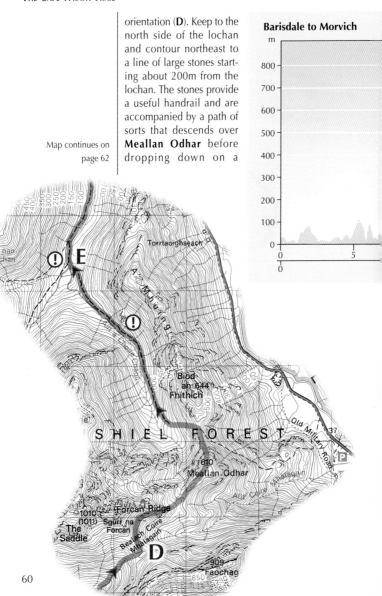

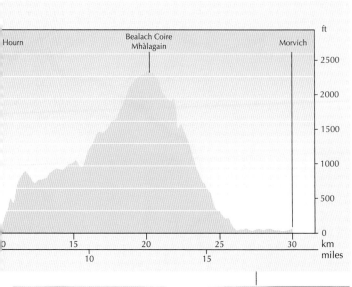

Forcan Ridge

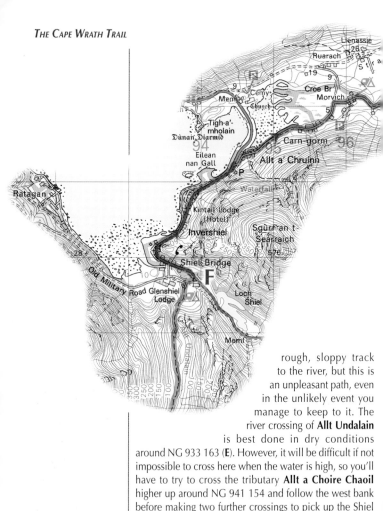

rough, sloppy track to the river, but this is an unpleasant path, even in the unlikely event you manage to keep to it. The river crossing of **Allt Undalain** is best done in dry conditions around NG 933 163 (**E**). However, it will be difficult if not impossible to cross here when the water is high, so you'll have to try to cross the tributary **Allt a Choire Chaoil** higher up around NG 941 154 and follow the west bank before making two further crossings to pick up the Shiel Brige path. Having crossed the river, you'll be glad to see the well defined path north to the A87 at **Shiel Bridge** (**F**).

◄ From the petrol station turn left and follow the A87 north along the shore of Loch Duich through Invershiel to the road junction at NG 944 202 to Morvich. Turn right and follow the road 1.5km northeast to **Morvich**.

Here there is a shop, campsite and petrol station.

Shiel Bridge, 3.4km southwest along the road from Morvich, has a reasonable range of amenities, including a small shop (at the petrol station), a hotel and bunkhouse, campsites and a youth hostel (at Ratagan). It is also the first point at which it's possible to escape via a bus service to Inverness.

Route alternatives

In foul weather, or if you are finding the rough terrain particularly challenging this early in the walk, you have the option to take the road into Shiel Bridge. As you descend from Meallan Odhar to Bealach na Craoibhe, turn east instead of heading west and descend to the A87. ▶

It's a long old slog and a relatively busy road, so this alternative really should be used only in emergencies.

Looking back to Sgurr na Creige from Shiel Bridge

ALTERNATIVE STAGE 1
Fort William to Laggan

Start	Fort William
Finish	Laggan
Distance	41km (25½ miles)
Ascent	550m
Average duration	1–2 days
Terrain	Mostly easy along a mixture of towpaths, road and good forest tracks
Maps	OS Landranger 41 (Ben Nevis); 34 (Fort Augustus): OS Explorer 392 (Ben Nevis & Fort William); 400 (Loch Lochy & Glen Roy)
Amenities	Hostels (Banavie, Gairlochy and Laggan); B&B (South Laggan); shop (Well of the Seven Heads, Laggan)
Camping	Some good spots on the shore of Loch Lochy north of Clunes

This popular alternative start to the trail comprises three stages and rejoins the main route at Morvich (near Shiel Bridge). Starting along this route also gives you more chance to vary the route to the east, whereas the main route tends to hug the west coast. However, the start of this route alternative could scarcely be less prepossessing. As you cross the supermarket car park, the most pressing danger is being mown down by frantic shoppers jockeying for parking spaces. But it reminds you of the urban landscape you're leaving behind for the next few weeks.

The first three miles are also pretty grim as the route snakes out of Fort William along the Great Glen Way, through a housing estate and along a grubby shoreline towards Banavie. If you're not a purist, you might decide to start your journey from Banavie itself (one stop from Fort William on the train). The Great Glen Way is now your guide all the way to Laggan. This stage will delight canal aficionados, as it follows the Caledonian Canal towpath directly to Loch Lochy. An advantage to this route alternative is that the going is easier for the first couple of days giving legs, feet and shoulders time to adjust to the trail and a rucksack. There is good hostel accommodation in Banavie, Gairlochy and Laggan. On a fine day there will be superb views across to the Aonachs, Carn Mor Dearg and the brutal mass of Ben Nevis's northeast buttress jutting into the skyline.

From the main entrance of the train station at Fort William, turn right and cross the Morrison's car park to pick up the start of the **Great Glen Way** just to the left of the McDonald's drive through restaurant.

Map continues on
page 66

65

THE CAPE WRATH TRAIL

The **Great Glen Way (GGW)** is a popular National Trail in its own right. It runs for 73 miles between Fort William and Inverness, following a geological fault line connecting Loch Ness, Loch Oich and Loch Lochy and effectively dividing northern and southern Scotland. Being an official long distance path, it's well waymarked with blue posts so your navigational skills shouldn't be put to the test just yet.

Distinctive marker posts, Great Glen Way

Follow GGW way-marks along the back of the shinty stadium, through the **Caol** housing estate and around the shoreline of Loch Linnhe to the towpath of the **Caledonian Canal**. Once you pick up the towpath, follow it towards Banavie.

Map continues below

At Banavie **Neptune's Staircase**, an impressive series of eight locks, brings Thomas Telford's Caledonian Canal 18 metres down to sea level at Loch Linnhe. The canal links the lochs en route and when completed in 1822 allowed vessels to cross from the Atlantic to the North Sea for the first time.

Map continues on page 68

From **Banavie**, continue along the towpath, past the locks of **Neptune's Staircase** (**A**) for just over 11km to **Gairlochy** (**B**).

At Gairlochy, cross to the west side of the canal and continue to follow the GGW waymarks to **Clunes** (**C**) along a short stretch of

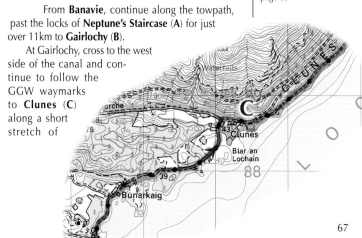

Map continues opposite

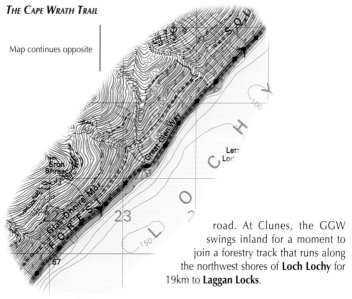

road. At Clunes, the GGW
swings inland for a moment to
join a forestry track that runs along
the northwest shores of **Loch Lochy** for
19km to **Laggan Locks**.

Route alternatives

If you're hankering to get off the beaten track sooner,
you might consider leaving the Great Glen Way at Clunes
and following the B8005 5km west to Achnasaul. From
here a good track heads north, skirting Glas Bheinn
before climbing over rough, trackless ground to Bealach

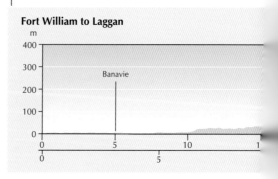

Fort William to Laggan

carn na h-Urchaire. From here descend northeast to pick up a rough track that heads north and then northeast over Meall Tarsuinn, before descending into the Glengarry forest to meet the main route at Garrygualach. Another option that 'cuts the corner', avoiding Invergarry, is the track that heads west from the South Laggan Forest at NN 251 936 before heading north to the main route in Glengarry forest.

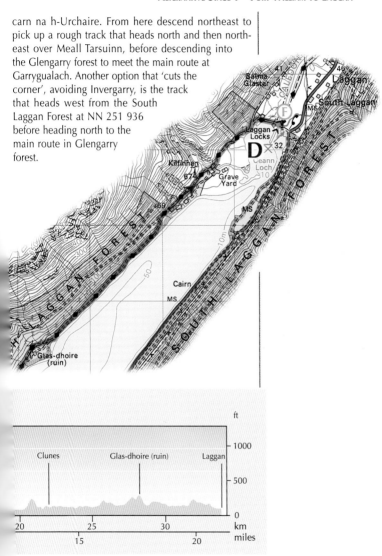

ALTERNATIVE STAGE 2
Laggan to Cluanie

Start	Laggan
Finish	Cluanie
Distance	44.7km (27¾ miles)
Ascent	1190m
Average duration	1–2 days
Terrain	Initially easy along forest tracks, before becoming rough and boggy as you climb towards Glen Loyne
Maps	OS Landranger 34 (Fort Augustus): OS Explorer 400 (Loch Lochy & Glen Roy); 415 (Glen Affric & Glen Morriston)
Amenities	Hotels (Invergarry, Cluanie)
Camping	Options are limited. Some riverside possibilities near Loch Garry west of Garrygualach. Glen Loyne looks promising on the map, but is too rough and boggy for riverside camping. Some good, sheltered spots in the small corrie at Creag Liathtais. Some flat spots by the bridge over Loch Cluanie, but close to the busy road so hardly idyllic.

This is very much a stage of two halves. The first half continues in the same vein as the previous stage, with easy walking along wide forest tracks. The second half provides the first tantalising taste of wildness. If you're strong and fit the initial walking is easy enough to mean you could do this stage in one long push, but it makes for a very long day. At the outset you'll have the familiar blue posts of the Great Glen Way to guide you, but these are soon left behind and are the last waymarks you'll see on this trip. The section through Glengarry Forest is pleasant, if somewhat uninspiring. As with so many managed forestry areas, dense uniform stands of pine alternate with areas of utter devastation where the trees have been razed by logging.

On the other side of Loch Garry, the Tomdoun Lodge Hotel has long been a popular point of rest and refreshment, but at the time of writing is up for sale. Leaving the forestry of Glengarry, you climb the slopes of an area marked as East Glenquoich Forest, notable now for the complete absence of trees, but once part of the original, native Caledonian Forest.

Map continues on page 73

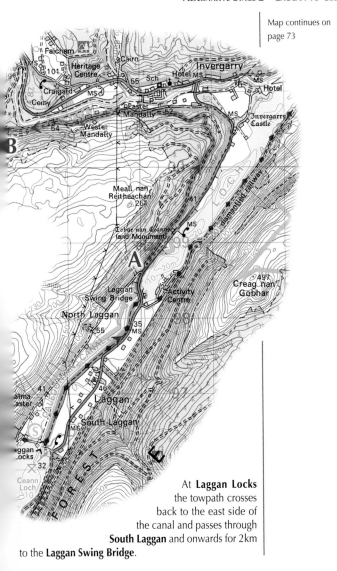

At **Laggan Locks** the towpath crosses back to the east side of the canal and passes through **South Laggan** and onwards for 2km to the **Laggan Swing Bridge**.

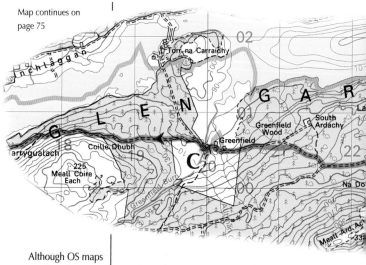

Map continues on page 75

Although OS maps show the GGW following the east side of the loch, it is waymarked here.

Cross the Laggan Swing Bridge to the west side of the canal and follow the A82 for about half a kilometre before branching off left onto a forestry track at NN 301 987 (**A**). ◀ Stay on the main forest track as

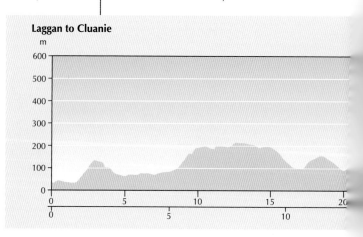

Laggan to Cluanie

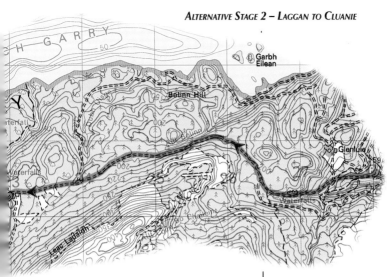

it climbs up through woods before dropping back down to a small road at NH 300 007, where you part company with the GGW and its way-marks. Follow the road west, ignoring diverging tracks. After 2km the road becomes a good forestry track (**B**) that

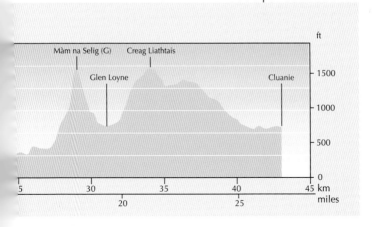

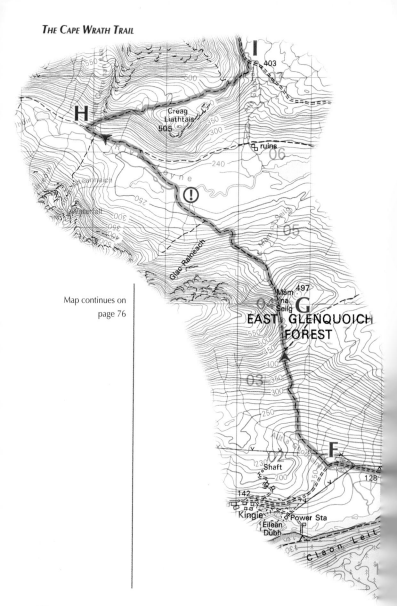

Map continues on
page 76

leads west for 7km through the **Glengarry Forest** to a path junction at NH 216 003. Take the right fork and continue for a further 5km past the buildings at **Greenfield** (**C**) to **Garrygualach** (**D**). From here, the path continues west along the banks of the **River Garry** for 3.5km before turning uphill to a footbridge (**E**) and descending to cross the River Garry just east of **Eilean a Mhorair** at NH 133 011. Once you've crossed the bridge, climb briefly to the road and follow it west for 2km before turning northwest onto a rough but well defined footpath (**F**) at NH 113 019 that climbs up for 2.5km to the pass at **Màm na Selig** (**G**) before descending into Glen Loyne.

EAST GLENQUOICH FOREST AND GLEN LOYNE

The area marked on the maps as as East Glenquoich Forest was part of the original Caledonian Forest, native woods that once covered more than 1.5 million hectares (6000 square miles) of the Highlands. A true mosaic of tree species, the ancient forest included scots pine, aspen, birch, oak, rowan, holly, willow and alder – a far cry from the serried ranks of spruce common in modern commercial plantations. A combination of climate change, over-grazing and logging has left only one per cent of the original forest standing.

Glen Loyne itself has a feeling of eerie remoteness enhanced by the gnarled grey branches of the few remaining Scots pines, hunched on the southern slopes of the glen. These last surviving trees are thought to include one that is 550 years old, the oldest in Scotland. As you descend towards the River Loyne, you'll cross a new, fenced area. Cast your eyes down and all

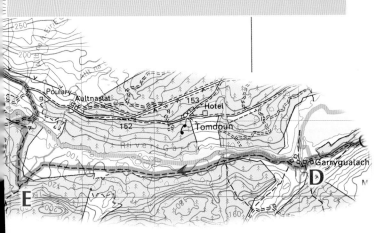

around you'll see young saplings, poking through the bog and heather. These are part of a concerted effort to restore more than 234,000 hectares (900 square miles) of land to native forest. It's hard not to wonder what a majestic addition these will be to the barren slopes of Glen Loyne in decades to come. But for now, you can enjoy the first proper taste of remoteness, and the first chance to get your feet wet crossing the bogs and river.

Descend from the pass down into Glen Loyne, traversing an area of new forestry that is surrounded by a high deer fence. Crossing the **River Loyne** is difficult when in spate, but in most conditions will be relatively straightforward around the point marked on the OS map. Once you have crossed the river, pick up the path on the north bank which climbs to intersect another path heading northwest at NH 086 060. Follow this path for just under a kilometre, crossing **Allt Coire nan Leac**, to a junction at NH 079 063 (**H**). Climb northeast between **Creag a'Mhàim** and **Creag Liathtais** for 2km before descending to join a 4x4 track at NH 101 072 (**I**), which descends for 6km to **Cluanie**.

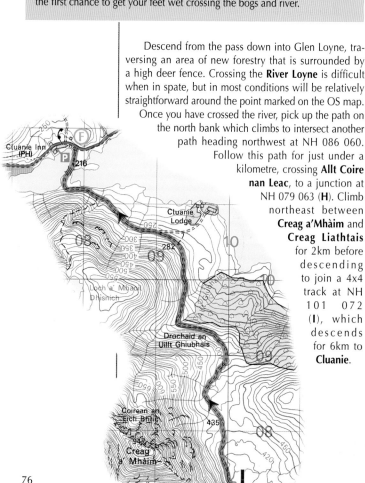

ALTERNATIVE STAGE 3

Cluanie to Morvich (near Shiel Bridge)

Start	Cluanie
Finish	Morvich
Distance	26.6km (16½ miles)
Ascent	730m
Average Duration	1 day
Terrain	Clearly defined tracks, but rough and boggy in many places
Maps	OS Landranger 34 (Fort Augustus); 33 (Loch Alsh & Glen Shiel); 25 (Glen Carron): OS Explorer 414 (Glen Shiel & Kintail Forest); 415 Glen Affric & Glen Morriston
Amenities	Camban bothy (NH 053 184); youth hostel (Alltbeithe); shop, hotel, bunkhouse, B&Bs (Shiel Bridge)
Camping	Campsites (Shiel Bridge); excellent riverside camping opportunities abound

The terrain on this stage is some of the finest of the whole route. It is almost entirely devoid of roads and retains a real sense of remoteness. The hostel at Alltbeithe is one of the remotest in the country and beyond here there is great potential for route variations. The main route steers via Morvich to take advantage of the amenities there, and in nearby Shiel Bridge, but you may prefer to stay out in the wilds and there are several good options to consider. The difference to the well trodden Great Glen Way is immediately apparent and it's easy to go entire days without seeing another soul. Of course, such remoteness requires good equipment, experience and preparation.

From the hotel at **Cluanie** turn right along the road for 1.5km. ▶ At NH 092 121 turn left onto a clear path (**A**) that runs along **An Caorann Mòr** for 9km into Glen Affric to the **Alltbeithe youth hostel**. The path becomes rougher and less distinct the further you progress (**B**): try to keep to the higher path, avoiding dropping down too close to

This is a busy, fast road with no pavement, so take care.

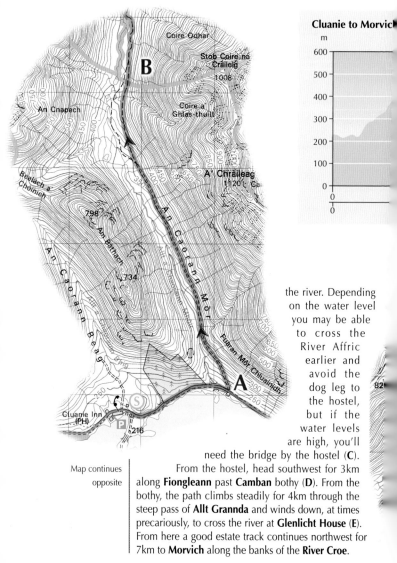

Cluanie to Morvich

m

600

500

400

300

200

100

0

0

0

the river. Depending on the water level you may be able to cross the River Affric earlier and avoid the dog leg to the hostel, but if the water levels are high, you'll need the bridge by the hostel (**C**).

From the hostel, head southwest for 3km along **Fiongleann** past **Camban** bothy (**D**). From the bothy, the path climbs steadily for 4km through the steep pass of **Allt Grannda** and winds down, at times precariously, to cross the river at **Glenlicht House** (**E**). From here a good estate track continues northwest for 7km to **Morvich** along the banks of the **River Croe**.

Map continues opposite

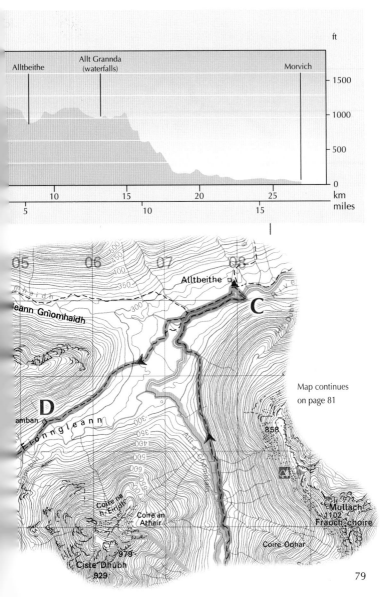

Map continues
on page 81

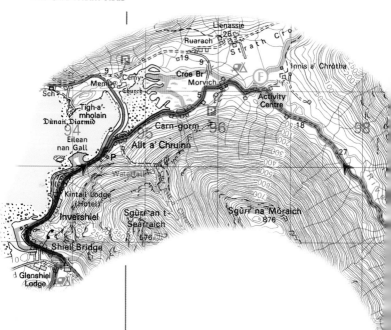

Nearby Shiel Bridge has a reasonable range of amenities, including a small shop (at the petrol station), a hotel and bunkhouse, campsites and a youth hostel (at Ratagan). From here it's possible to escape via a bus service to Inverness.

Route alternatives

This stage loops west to Morvich to link back to the main route and take advantage of the amenities in Morvich and Shiel Bridge, should they be needed. But if your schedule allows more flexibility, from Alltbeithe youth hostel you could head up Gleann Gnìomhaidh to the stunning Loch a Bhealaich. ◀ The path can then be followed north to meet up with the main route at Carnach. The

This is one of the most beautiful and remote glens in Scotland.

more adventurous (and experienced) might even consider a climb north from the youth hostel to Stob Coire na Cloiche, followed by a short ridge walk east to intercept the path at Bealach Coire Ghàidhail that descends north along Gleann a' Choilich to the shores of Loch Mullardoch, before turning west to pick up the main route at Iron Lodge.

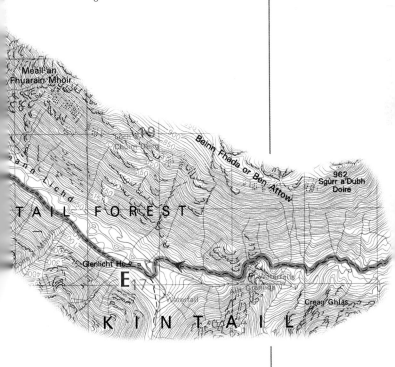

STAGE 5
Morvich (near Shiel Bridge) to Strathcarron

Start	Morvich
Finish	Strathcarron
Distance	38.7km (24 miles)
Ascent	1370m
Average duration	2 days
Terrain	Good, clear paths initially, tricky descent from falls of Glomach to River Elchaig. Ground between Iron Lodge and Bendronaig Lodge can be boggy with many river crossings
Maps	OS Landranger 33 (Loch Alsh, Glen Shiel & Loch Hourn); 25 (Glen Carron & Glen Affric); OS Explorer 413 (Knoydart, Loch Hourn & Loch Duich); 414 (Glen Shiel & Kintail Forest); 429 (Glen Carron & West Monar); Harvey Superwalker Kintail (Glen Shiel)
Amenities	Maol Bhuidhe bothy (NH 052 360); Bendroniag Lodge estate bothy (NH 014 389); Strathcarron Hotel (Strathcarron)
Camping	Some spots by the river at the top of the falls and by the River Elchaig. Other possibilities towards Maol-buidhe by Allt na Sean-luibe or by the River Ling, around Bendronaig Lodge, Lochan Fuara and at the Strathcarron Hotel (with permission).

This is one of the most spectacular stages of the walk and there are many possible routes. Shiel Bridge itself, huddled on the edge of Loch Duich in the shadow of the imposing Five Sisters of Kintail is a pretty special place to spend a while. But the trail takes you inexorably forward and from Bealach na Sròine you descend past the impressive Falls of Glomach.

This is rough country, so don't underestimate the time it will take you to cover the distance. Once you reach the River Elchaig you have a route choice to make (see route alternatives). The main route turns east to Iron Lodge before heading north to Maol-bhuidhe bothy (a convenient overnight stop). Despite the more direct route alternatives, this is some of the wildest, most unspoilt country in Scotland so it seems a shame to skirt it. From Maol-bhuidhe the track heads north then east around Beinn Dronaig before passing the well-appointed estate bothy at Bendronaig Lodge (it even has a flushing toilet!). From Bendronaig the path continues east heading up and over Creag Dubh Bheag before dropping down to Strathcarron. Here there is a welcoming hotel where you can also camp (with permission) and a train station on the Inverness to Skye line, but not much else. If you're doing the trail in sections, it's a good break point and marks the end of the first section.

From **Morvich**, turn right along a minor road that passes the caravan and campsite. Continue along this road past the activity centre to its end and then pick up a footpath, signposted to the Falls of Glomach.

Map continues on page 84

The footpath runs along the southwest bank of the river for 1.5km to a wooden post that marks the short descent to the bridge at NG 981 223 (**A**). The path then climbs briefly from the bridge through woods to a gate. From the gate, turn right and then head north up through the Dorusdain Wood (the path continues to be signposted for the Falls of Glomach), crossing another bridge over the **Allt an Leòid Ghaineamhaich**.

83

Falls of Glomach

From here a clear path climbs steeply northeast over **Bealach na Sròine** to the **Falls of Glomach (B)**.

The **waterfall** here cascades more than 100m straight down into the ravine, the largest drop of any waterfall in the UK. The path can be quite tricky as it hangs on the west side of the gorge and goes over several awkward rock steps. In poor visibility or wind, proceed with caution. The way down gradually becomes less treacherous, but care is still needed.

At the top of the falls, the most obvious path descends to a viewpoint 25m or so below. The path you're looking for is more faint and roughly follows the contours from the wooden danger sign and a large boulder, skirting under a prominent crag. Following this path takes you down the side of the ravine, precariously over several narrow and rocky sections – take great care here as a slip could be dangerous.

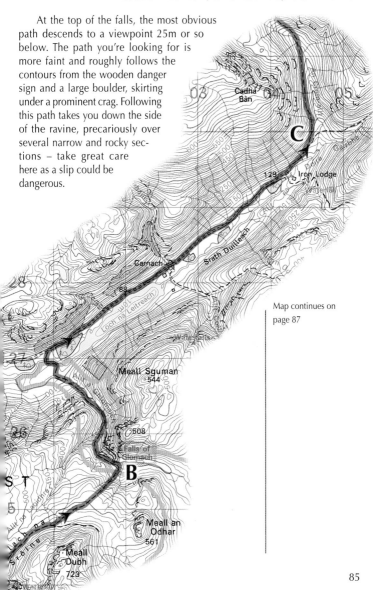

Map continues on page 87

85

Some bank erosion has taken place around the ford at NH 017 261, which could make the tributary difficult to cross in spate.

◀ From here a clear path descends to cross the River Elchaig via two foot bridges. On the other side of the river, a wide 4x4 track heads east along the shores of **Loch na Leitreach** towards **Carnach**, where there are a few small dwellings and a hunting lodge. Continue on the 4x4 track past another building, **Iron Lodge**, before turning north along **An Crom-allt** (**C**), climbing past a potentially difficult ford at NH 044 311 and continuing north along the glen on a clear but boggy path for 5km before reaching the bothy at **Maol-bhuidhe** (**D**), set in a stunning location on the shores of **Loch Cruoshie**.

From the bothy, head due north and ford the **River Ling** where safest, before turning west and contouring around the southern slopes of **Beinn Dronaig**. There's no path at first, but as you climb, you'll pick up a faint stalker's track (**E**) around NH 011 368 that descends to the excellent bothy at **Bendronaig Lodge**, maintained by the estate. From Bendroniag Lodge, take the 4x4 track that follows the river east to a bridge. Stay on the main track

Glen Ling

Map continues on
page 88

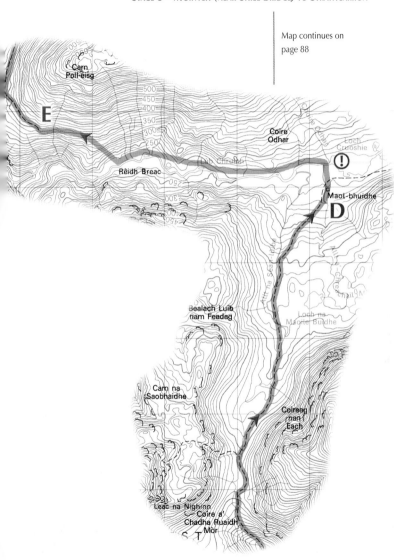

Carn
Poll-eisg

E

Coire
Odhar

Loch
Cruoshie

500
450
400
350
300
250

Dub Chruinn

Rèidh Breac

250

Maol-bhuidhe

(!)

D

300

400

Allt na Sean-luibe

Bealach Luib
nam Feadag

Loch na
Maoile Buidhe

an
Cheann
Chail M

Carn na
Saobhaidhe

Coireag
nan
Each

Leac na Nighinn
Còire a'
Chadha Ruaidh
Mòr

S T

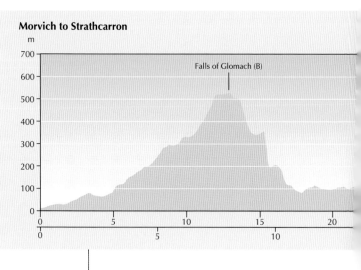

Morvich to Strathcarron

Falls of Glomach (B)

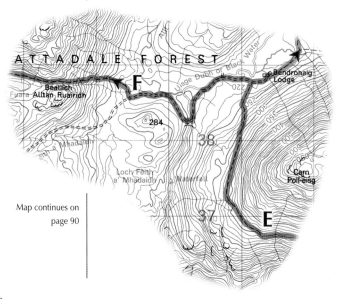

A T T A D A L E   F O R E S T

Bealach
Fuara Alltan Ruairidh

Uisge Dubh or Black Water

Bendronaig
Lodge

284

38

Allt a' Mhadaidh

Loch Féith
a' Mhadaidh

Waterfall

Carn
Poll-eisg

Map continues on
page 90

37

F

E

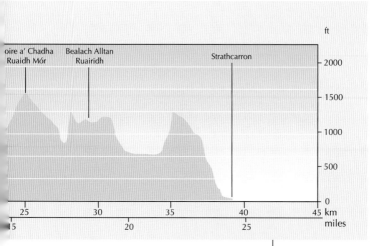

for another kilometre beyond the bridge, but look out for a smaller path branching off to the right at NG 994 385 (**F**). This is a clear but roughish path that climbs steadily to the pass at **Bealach Alltan Ruairidh**, before descending to the north of **Lochan Fuara** and continuing for 5km to the road at **Achintee** a short distance south of Strathcarron.

Route alternatives

This stage provides the most opportunities to stray from the 'main' route. For instance, after descending from the Falls of Glomach you could head west along the River Elchaig (where there are some good wild camping spots), passing Camus Luinie (where there is a bunkhouse) and Killilan before heading up Glen Ling and climbing northeast through the forest to pick up a 4x4 track that takes you on a dog leg towards Bendronaig Lodge. You could then rejoin the main route to Strathcarron around NH 995 386.

Previous guides have suggested descending to Attadale and then continuing to Strathcarron on the road. This is definitely not recommended. Occasional trains run from Attadale Station, but they are few and far between. The road is fast with several dangerous blind bends and should be avoided unless in an emergency.

If you follow the main route to Bendronaig Lodge, you could then head north to the wonderfully isolated Bearneas (where there is another bothy NH 021 431) before heading northeast to Bealach Bhearnais and descending to cross the river at Pollan Buidhe and then north to Craig. ◄ Looking at the map there is the temptation to avoid Craig and to take a much more direct route to Achnashellach by climbing directly from Bearneas via Baobh-bhacan Dubha, descending through the Achnashellach Forest to the river. The river is the main problem with this alternative. There's no bridge and it's wide and difficult to cross in most circumstances. For this reason, this alternative is not recommended.

This alternative is described in more depth in Alternative stage 6.

2 STRATHCARRON TO INVERLAEL (NEAR ULLAPOOL)
80.2km, 3–4 days

Waterfall in Easan Dorcha (Alternative Stage 6)

2 STRATHCARRON TO INVERLAEL
(NEAR ULLAPOOL)

Coire Dubh Mor, Beinn Eighe

The middle section of the trail is the shortest and perhaps the easiest, but is still by no means straightforward. Much of this section follows good paths and offers a brief respite from the rugged, trackless terrain that characterises most of the route. When you reach the Ullapool road at Inverlael, you'll have a choice to make whether to divert via Ullapool to re-supply or continue along the trail.

STAGE 6
Strathcarron to Kinlochewe

Start	Strathcarron
Finish	Kinlochewe
Distance	34.7km (21½ miles)
Ascent	1110m
Average duration	1–2 days
Terrain	Mostly clear tracks, last section north of Beinn Eighe very rough and trackless
Maps	OS Landranger 25 (Glen Carron & Glen Affric): OS Explorer 429 (Glen Carron & West Monar)
Amenities	Coire Fionnaraich bothy (NG 950 480); youth hostel (Torridon); campsite (Taggan NH 014 636); Post Office, café, shop, hotel, bunkhouse, B&Bs (Kinlochewe)
Camping	Bealach Ban, good flat spots by A896 in Glen Torridon past the Ling Hut, otherwise limited due to rough ground

This is a superb and challenging stage of the trail that starts out gently enough as you wind along the River Carron on a new path created for fishermen, passing the various named beats. This brings you to within a stone's throw of Coulags where you head north, following the Fionn-abhainn river. You'll pass a well kept bothy (Coire Fionnaraich NG 950 480) as you ascend past Loch Coire Fionnaraich to Bealach Ban. From here you descend into the majestic Glen Torridon passing the famous Ling Hut (a private climbers' place) and cross the A896 that scythes through the glen.

This stage of the walk can be accomplished by strong walkers in a day, but others might choose to break it up. Beware the sting in the tail as the last section in the shadow of Beinn Eighe is spectacular, but rough. It is suggested as the main route because of the sheer quality of the country around Beinn Eighe, but there are several options to make this stage easier (see route alternatives) or provide an escape route into Kinlochewe in bad weather. Kinlochewe itself is a small village with some backpacker friendly facilities. The hotel has a bunkhouse and there are several good B&Bs and a basic campsite at Taggan. There's also a Post Office and small shop (the petrol station also sells some provisions) making it a good place to re-stock or collect a supply parcel. Buses stop at the hotel connecting to Inverness.

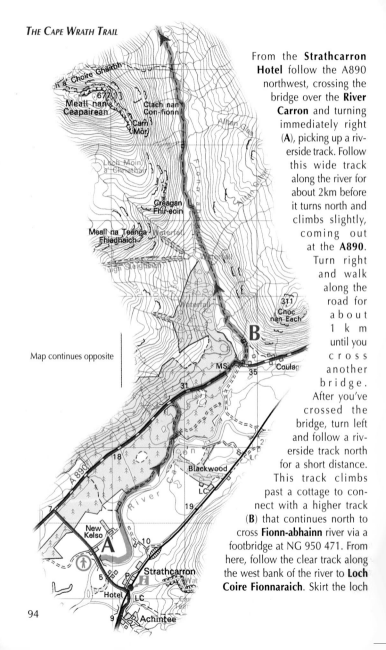

From the **Strathcarron Hotel** follow the A890 northwest, crossing the bridge over the **River Carron** and turning immediately right (**A**), picking up a riverside track. Follow this wide track along the river for about 2km before it turns north and climbs slightly, coming out at the **A890**. Turn right and walk along the road for about 1 k m until you cross another bridge. After you've crossed the bridge, turn left and follow a riverside track north for a short distance. This track climbs past a cottage to connect with a higher track (**B**) that continues north to cross **Fionn-abhainn** river via a footbridge at NG 950 471. From here, follow the clear track along the west bank of the river to **Loch Coire Fionnaraich**. Skirt the loch

Map continues opposite

Bothy at Coire Fionnaraich, near Strathcarron

and climb on a faint path that contours round **Coire Fionnaraich**, ascending to **Bealach Ban**.

Once you enter the bealach the path becomes difficult to follow, but continue northeast as best you can and then descend over rough ground (you'll need to use a bearing in poor visibility). You'll find that a faint path re-appears around NG 950 525 (C) and gets steadily better as you descend north into Glen Torridon to the **Ling Hut** and the **A896** road. But for this human intrusion, you are alone in the heart of one of the finest mountainous areas in the world.

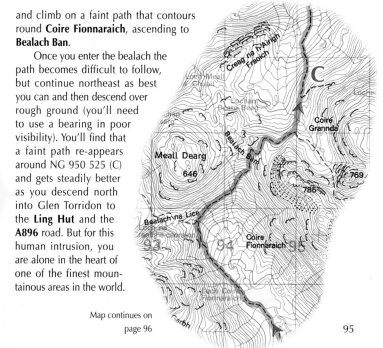

Map continues on page 96

95

There are superb, unspoilt views of the wonderful glens all around you – this is Torridon proper and one of the highlights of the trail.

Once you hit the road, turn left and cross the river over the road bridge before taking a clear track north from the other side of the bridge that climbs into **Coire Dubh Mòr** along the west bank of the river. After about 2km, cross the river at NG 946 589 and continue climbing northeast, contouring around **Sàil Mhòr**. You'll pass two path junctions, and in each case you should take the right fork. This path continues to contour round Sàil Mhòr becoming increasingly faint and hard to follow. ◄

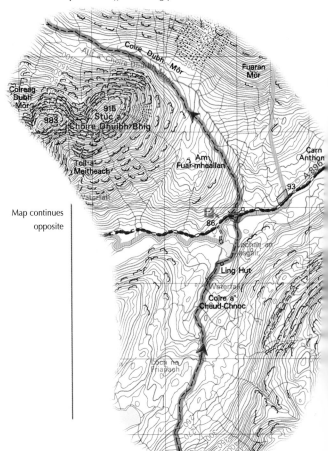

Map continues opposite

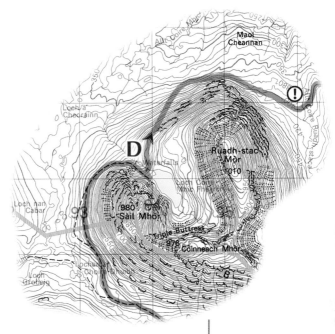

You'll pass near the place where in March 1951 **a Lancaster bomber crashed** near the summit of Beinn Eighe. All eight crew from RAF Kinloss died. Difficulties in recovering the bodies led to the formation of RAF Mountain Rescue which exists to this day. A small brass plaque on part of the wreckage commemorates the accident and the area is known as Fuselage Gully.

In a strange twist to the story in 2008, a climber's fall during an avalanche was broken by a propeller from the plane, he was injured but survived the incident.

Cross the river flowing from **Loch Coire Mhic Fhearchair** below the waterfalls (this will be difficult in spate) (**D**) and descend from here to pick up the 400m

Map continues on page 98

97

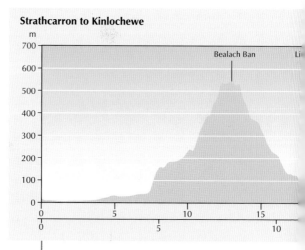

Strathcarron to Kinlochewe

Bealach Ban

contour (there's no path). The 400m contour provides a useful guide rail to take you round the flanks of **Ruadh-stac Mòr**, and in poor visibility a GPS may be useful here as the terrain is quite disorientating. Using the 400m contour as your guide, cross the **Allt Coire Ruadh-staca** river (this will be another difficult crossing in spate). ◄ After crossing the river continue to follow the 400m contour east for about 2.5km to the pass at NG 984 624 (**E**). From

Try to avoid dropping too low at all costs as it will take you into some horrible, rough, boggy ground.

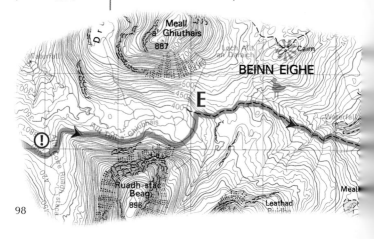

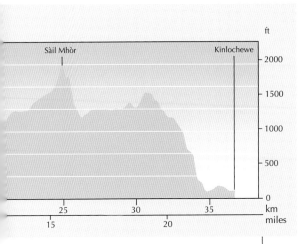

here you'll pick up a clear path that you'll be very glad to see. It descends east for 3km to woodland. On entering the woods, turn right and follow a path for 1km that leads directly into **Kinlochewe**.

Route alternatives

The main route alternative on this stage is via Achnashellach. ▶ The hard section beyond the Ling Hut can be cut out by diverting east from Bealach Bàn, skirting Sgorr nan Lochan Uaine and descending to pick up a path at Coire an Leth-uillt. This path leads to Coulin Lodge, from where a 4x4 track heads southeast for a couple of kilometres to intersect Alternative Stage 6.

To access this alternative, you'll either need to use Alternative Stage 6 or continue along the A890 past Coulags to join this alternative at Achnashellach.

99

ALTERNATIVE STAGE 6
Bendronaig to Kinlochewe

Start	Bendronaig
Finish	Kinlochewe
Distance	37.8km (23½ miles)
Ascent	1100m
Average duration	1–2 days
Terrain	Rough, boggy challenging country to Craig, but good paths thereafter
Maps	OS Landranger 19 (Gairloch & Ullapool); 25 (Glen Carron & Glen Affric): OS Explorer 414 (Glen Shiel & Kintail Forest); 429 (Glen Carron & West Monar)
Amenities	Bernais bothy (NH 021 431); Easan Dorcha bothy (NH 012 526); hostel (Achnashellach) (01520 766232); B&Bs, hotel, bunkhouse, shop, café, Post Office (Kinlochewe)
Camping	Good spots in Pollan Buidhe and Easan Dorcha

From Bendronaig Lodge, a tempting alternative is to head north to the wonderfully isolated Bearneas bothy before turning northeast to Bealach Bhearnais and descending to cross the river at Pollan Buidhe and then north to Craig (home to the legendary Gerry's hostel). Looking at the map there is the temptation to avoid Craig and to take a much more direct route to Achnashellach by climbing directly from Bearneas via Baobh-bhacan Dubha before descending through the Achnashellach Forest to the river. The river is the problem with this alternative. It is wide and fast flowing and can be difficult to cross.

From Craig there's a short stretch of road towards Achnashellach before the route heads north towards Beinn Liath Mhor, down the idyllic Easan Dorcha (where there is another small hut/bothy) and northeast to Torran Cuilinn. From there, a climb through the forest and over Carn Dhomnhuill Mhic a' Ghobha takes you on a steady descent to Kinlochewe, through an area of felled forest, finishing along the river.

From **Bendronaig** bothy head north on a good track for 3km past **Loch an Laoigh**. From the loch the path turns northeast, becoming indistinct as you cross the rivers in **Coire Beithe**. Contour for 3km to **Bealach Bhearnais** (**A**) over rough track-less ground and descend from the bealach

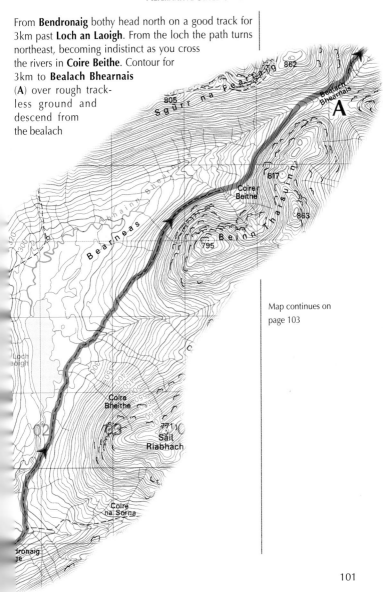

Map continues on page 103

Map continues on
page 104

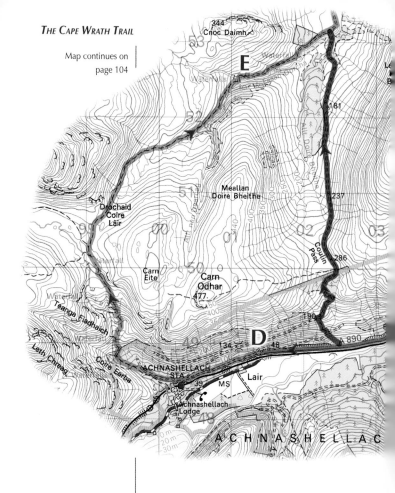

on a clear track northeast to cross the river in **Pollan Buidhe** (**B**). Once you've crossed the river, follow a wide 4x4 track on the east bank of the river that leads 4km to a bridge at NH 047 492. Cross the bridge and then turn left along a track that follows the railway line for a kilometre into **Craig** (**C**). From Craig follow the **A890** 2.5km west and then turn right onto a forest track at NH 016 488 (**D**).

This track runs west for 3km past the **train station** into **Coire Earba**, before climbing north into **Drochaid Coire Làir**. As you climb, bear right at the path junctions at NH 991 502. From Drochaid Coire Làir, follow the clear track that descends into **Easan Dorcha** (**E**), descending north-east then north along the banks of the river to **Coulin**. At Coulin, turn right and continue for 0.5km to the house at Torran-cuilinn (**F**).

Pass in front of the house and climb into the woods on a wide 4x4 track. After about 0.75km, and as you pass a fence line, look for a smaller path that climbs steeply north from around NH 022 556. Turn right and follow

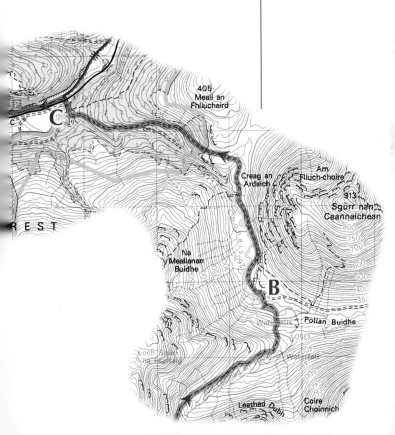

Bendronaig to Kinlochewe

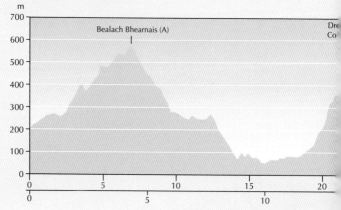

this clear path north out of the woods, contouring round **Carn Dhomnhuill Mhic a' Ghobha**. The path then descends to an area of woodland that has been felled, but is still marked on the OS maps (**G**). You can either skirt the boundary of the area or take one of the paths diagonally through the felled forestry. On leaving the forestry (**H**), cross the burn (Allt a Ghiuthais) around NH 026 602 and continue for 2km to **Kinlochewe**. ◄

The path is rough, overgrown and indistinct, so the best approach is to try to stay close to the river.

104   Map continues on page 106

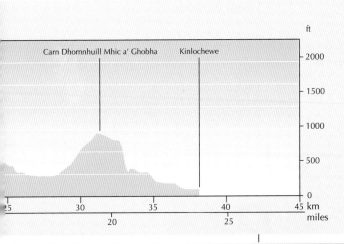

Carn Dhomnhuill Mhic a' Ghobha   Kinlochewe

ft
2000
1500
1000
500
0
25   30   35   40   45 km
        20   25   miles

Sunset towards Torran-cuilinn

Route alternatives

In bad conditions or if legs are suffering you could climb northwest from beyond Craig at NH 030 490 on a rough track to intersect a good 4x4 track due north to the Coulin Pass and onwards to join the main route at Torran-cuilinn. ◄ On reaching the area of felled forestry before Kinlochewe, you could descend to the bridge at NH 018 592 and take the road into Kinlochewe, avoiding the rough hack along the river.

Although more direct, this route is a lot less picturesque.

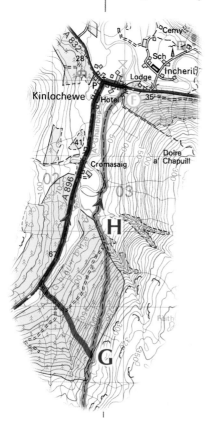

STAGE 7
Kinlochewe to Strath na Sealga

Start	Kinlochewe
Finish	Strath na Sealga
Distance	27.3km (17 miles)
Ascent	720m
Average duration	1 day
Terrain	Mainly clear paths, with a rough trackless section above Lochan Fada to Bealach Na Croise
Maps	OS Landranger 25 (Glen Carron); 19 (Gairloch & Ullapool): OS Explorer 429 (Glen Carron & West Monar); 433 (Torridon, Beinn Eighe & Liathach); 435 (An Teallach & Slioch): Harvey Superwalker Torridon
Amenities	Leckie bothy (NH 096 645); Shenavall bothy (NH 066 810)
Camping	By rivers Abhainn Bruachaig and Abhainn Gleann na Muice; by Loch an Nid; in Strath na Sealga

This stage offers some respite, but is still by no means easy. As you climb the wide, easy track that takes you quickly onwards up Gleann na Muice, enjoy the steady going while it lasts, it gets tougher from here on, but the good paths lead all the way to Lochan Fada.

From Lochan Fada you strike northeast, contouring to Bealach na Croise: dropping down will lead you into a world of boggy pain. From the bealach a reasonable stalker's path takes you to Loch an Nid. From here a rough but reasonably well defined path takes you all the way to Strath na Sealga and the superbly located bothy at Shenavall (NH 066 810). Going via Shenavall takes the route on a slight dog leg, but on a fine evening the views out to Loch na Sealga and of the impressive An Teallach ridge are among the trail's finest. If you're in a rush, there's an obvious way to cut the route short, but why hurry?

Leave **Kinlochewe** east on the **A832**, turning left towards **Incheril** and crossing the **Kinlochewe River**.

Map continues on
page 111

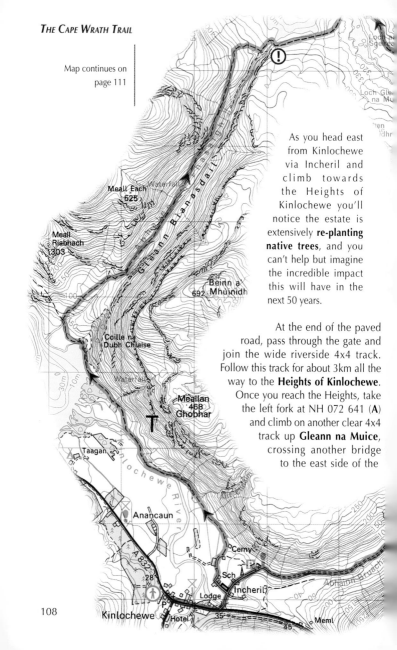

As you head east
from Kinlochewe
via Incheril and
climb towards
the Heights of
Kinlochewe you'll
notice the estate is
extensively **re-planting
native trees**, and you
can't help but imagine
the incredible impact
this will have in the
next 50 years.

At the end of the paved
road, pass through the gate and
join the wide riverside 4x4 track.
Follow this track for about 3km all the
way to the **Heights of Kinlochewe**.
Once you reach the Heights, take
the left fork at NH 072 641 (**A**)
and climb on another clear 4x4
track up **Gleann na Muice**,
crossing another bridge
to the east side of the

108

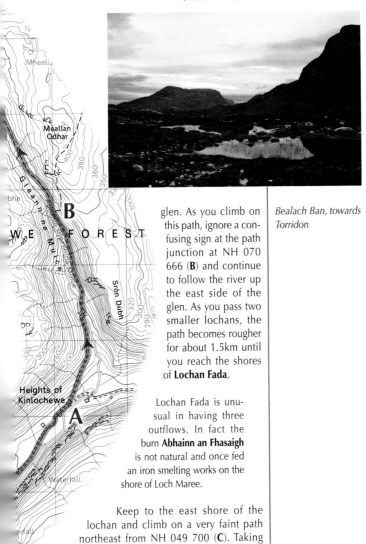

glen. As you climb on this path, ignore a confusing sign at the path junction at NH 070 666 (**B**) and continue to follow the river up the east side of the glen. As you pass two smaller lochans, the path becomes rougher for about 1.5km until you reach the shores of **Lochan Fada**.

Bealach Ban, towards Torridon

Lochan Fada is unusual in having three outflows. In fact the burn **Abhainn an Fhasaigh** is not natural and once fed an iron smelting works on the shore of Loch Maree.

Keep to the east shore of the lochan and climb on a very faint path northeast from NH 049 700 (**C**). Taking a bearing here is a good idea, even in clear

109

Kinlochewe to Strath na Sealga

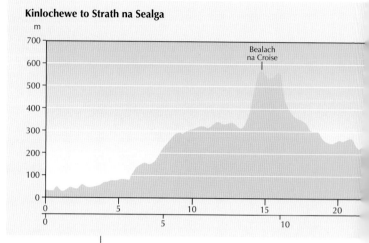

The ground is rough with no path and navigation will be tricky in poor visibility.

conditions. Although Loch Meallan an Fhudair makes a tempting navigational aid, it's best to stay higher as the ground below is very rough and boggy. ◀ Once you've crossed Coire Mhic Fhearchair, descend to **Bealach na Croise**, losing height and contouring gently.

Again, you'll need to watch your navigation here. A stalker's path not marked on OS is encountered around NH 071 719 (**D**) and descends for 2km to Loch an Nid.

Crossing the river here is tricky in spate but a shallow splash the rest of the time.

Cross the river close to where it flows into the loch. ◀ Pick up a clear path along the east side of **Abhainn Loch an Nid**. The path follows the shores of the loch for 1km and then the banks of the river for 4km to a junction with a bigger track at NH 090 787 (**E**). Turn left and head northwest into **Strath na Sealga** ◀ . As you follow the track, 3km along Strath na Sealga you'll pass several buildings before the path becomes increasingly rough as you approach the bothy at **Shenavall** (NH 066 810).

(turn right and climb for route alternative described below)

Route alternatives

The easy start to this stage is deliberate, but if you're after something a bit more challenging, you could head northwest from Incheril and climb Gleann Bianasdail to

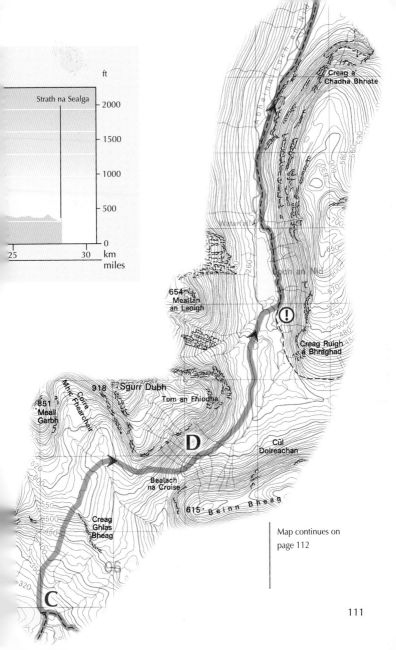

ft

Strath na Sealga

2000

1500

1000

500

0

25   30   km
                         miles

Creag a
Chadha Bhriste

Waterfall

Meallan
an Laoigh
654

Creag Ruigh
a Bhràghad

918 Sgurr Dubh
Tom an Fhiodha

Corie Mhic Fhearchair

851
Meall
Garbh

D

Cùl
Doireachan

Bealach
na Croise

615 Beinn Bheag

Creag
Ghlas
Bheag

Map continues on
page 112

C

rejoin the main route at Lochan Fada (the river crossing of Abhainn an Fhasaigh can be difficult). Another alternative heads north from Incheril along the shores of Loch Maree to Letterewe. From there you can climb to Bealach Mheinnidh and descend to cross Dubh Loch and Fionn Loch to Carnmore (where there is a barn that can be used for shelter). From there, the path heads west then northwest over the pass at Clach na Frithealaidh, descending into Gleann na Muice towards Larachantivore (a locked estate bothy). This is a superlative alternative for the hardy and experienced walker, but the route crosses several big rivers that come up very quickly in times of heavy rain, making them totally impassable. This is particularly true of the river in Strath na Sealga. ◄ If you want to cut out the dog leg to Shenavall, simply take the 4x4 track north from the path junction at NH 090 787 which climbs

If in any doubt don't try to cross, wait it out.

steeply and then descends to Corrie Hallie.

STAGE 8
Strath na Sealga to Inverlael (near Ullapool)

Start	Strath na Sealga
Finish	Inverlael
Distance	18.2km (11¼ miles)
Ascent	740m
Average duration	1 day
Terrain	A rough climb from Shenavall, a faint path climbing from Corrie Hallie and a steep slippery descent to Inverlael, but otherwise excellent paths
Maps	OS Landranger 19 (Gairloch & Ullapool); 20 (Ben Dearg & Loch Broom): OS Explorer 435 (An Teallach & Slioch); 436 (Beinn Dearg & Loch Fannich)
Amenities	Café and post box (Corrie Hallie); B&Bs (Dundonnell, Inverlael); numerous amenities (Ullapool)
Camping	Limited, some spots near the Dundonnell River, but section after Corrie Hallie generally too rough and boggy for camping

There are no truly easy stages of this walk but this one is a shorter and more forgiving than most. It's a tough start as you haul yourself up from Shenavall (assuming you stayed there or camped in Strath na Sealga). You'll be rewarded with stunning views of Loch na Sealga and the An Teallach ridge as you cross rough, boggy ground until you reach the 4x4 track that descends to Corrie Hallie. There's not much here except a post box and the possibility of tea and cake in the summer months. Dundonnell is relatively close and has some accommodation options.

A steep hack of a climb takes you up through farmland and woods to a clear but rough path over low and mainly featureless hills towards civilisation and the A835 to Ullapool. From here it's a kilometre north on the road to Inverlael. If you're planning to avoid Ullapool and stay in Inverlael, there are a few B&Bs relatively nearby. If you mention that you'll be arriving at Inverlael on foot, some will offer a collection and drop off service and save you a slog along the road.

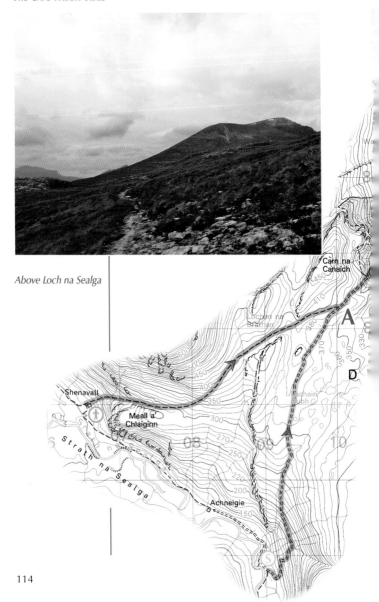

Above Loch na Sealga

Ascend from **Shenavall** to pick up a path above the bothy that climbs steeply beside Allt a Chlaiginn. Once you reach the top of the gully, the rough, boggy path continues northeast for 2km past **Lochan na Bràthan** to meet

Map continues on page 117

Fine views of the An Teallach ridge reward you for a tough start

the wide 4x4 track at NH 100 822 (**A**). You'll be glad to see the 4x4 track which descends for 3km to the road at **Corrie Hallie**. Once you hit the road, turn left and follow the road for 0.75km.

Look out for a right turn (signed Badralloch with a post box on the corner) and follow this road to cross the bridge over the **Dundonnell River** (**B**). Immediately after you've crossed the bridge, turn off the main road and pass through a gate on your right. Follow this track (it looks like more of a driveway) for 200m and where the track bends to the left, pass through a corner gate to the right into a field. Ascend diagonally across the field into woodland, joining a faint path that is unclear and overgrown. Ascend on this path through the wood for 0.75km before passing through a gate in the fence and leaving the wood. Continue on a clearer path to another fence and gate and then for another 0.5km to a **waterfall** (**C**). You'll need to be careful crossing the river here, don't do so at the first opportunity as this will bring you across too low. Instead,

Looking back to Beinn a Chlaidheimh

Strath na Sealga to Inverlael

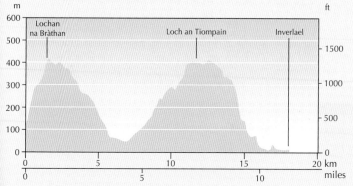

climb beside the river for 50m or so until you see the main track on the other side. Once you've crossed the river, the path onwards is reasonably well defined and climbs for 4.5km over the top of the hill and skirts by two small lochans (**D**). About 1km past the lochans, you'll pass through another gate and begin descending. ▶ Take the left fork at the path junction at NH 175 834 (**E**).

The path is steep and slippery.

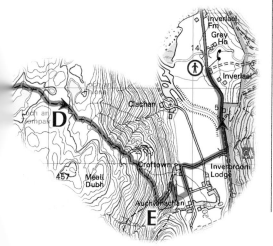

117

From here descend towards the edge of a stand of pine trees. The path follows the edge of the woodland before doubling back and descending through the woods to a gate. Go through the gate and cross the field diagonally northeast to a small road. Turn left and follow the road to **Croftown** before turning right to **Inverbroom** bridge, where the small road meets the **A835**. Walk 1km north on the A835 to **Inverlael**. ◄

There's no pavement, only a verge of sorts, and fast-moving traffic, so take care.

ULLAPOOL OPTIONS

Ullapool is a natural halfway point on the trail and makes a good spot to re-stock, rest or break the route. Hitting the tarmac at the A835 brings you back to civilisation with a jolt and presents a dilemma. Do you stay on the main route or divert to Ullapool? The town has a decent range of accommodation, a fair selection of shops and restaurants and a beautiful location, strung along the shore of Loch Broom. But with sufficient supplies you could simply continue from Inverlael towards Oykel Bridge, spurning civilisation altogether.

If you choose to visit Ullapool, the only way to get there (now that the ferry that used to make the crossing from the Altnaharrie Inn no longer oper-ates) is to brave a long slog (11.3km, 7 miles) along the A835 (there are no bus stops). There is a verge, but not much pavement, and big lorries thunder past at regular intervals, making the walk a hair-raising experience for pur-ists only. If there's any chance you may be walking the road in twilight or darkness, make sure you have appropriate reflective gear. I've done it once and would never want to do it again. A better option might be to call a taxi from Ullapool to collect you from the roadside at Inverlael (the phone box marked on OS has a car park next to it which is a good landmark). The taxi fare is around £15; arrange it in advance with Ewen's (01854 612966). The locals are a friendly bunch so you could also try your hand at hitchhiking. On your return, buses travelling out of Ullapool will usually stop at Inverlael on request. Instead of returning to Inverlael you could use Alternative Stage 9, which leaves from the back of Ullapool and winds pleasantly along the Ullapool and Rhidorroch rivers before rejoining the main route near Knockdamph bothy (NH 286 954).

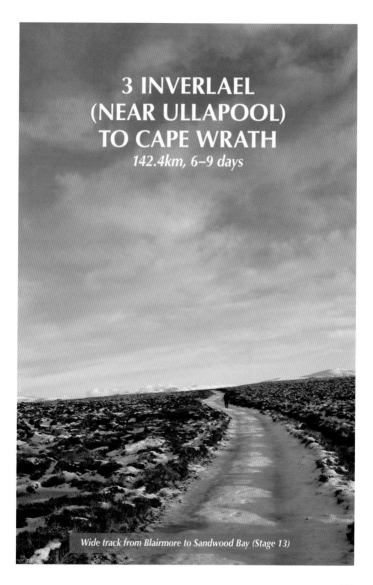

3 INVERLAEL
(NEAR ULLAPOOL)
TO CAPE WRATH
142.4km, 6–9 days

Wide track from Blairmore to Sandwood Bay (Stage 13)

3 INVERLAEL (NEAR ULLAPOOL) TO CAPE WRATH

Am Buachaille, Sandwood Bay

From the idyllic banks of the River Oykel, the ruggedness of Ben More, the super-lative sea lochs of Glencoul and Glendhu, Sandwood Bay, and then the wildness of the cape itself, the walk keeps some of its best moments until the final section. By now you'll be mentally and physically tired, but the majesty of the surroundings will keep you going.

STAGE 9

Inverlael (near Ullapool) to Oykel Bridge

Start	Inverlael
Finish	Oykel Bridge
Distance	33.5km (20¾ miles)
Ascent	840m
Average duration	1–2 days
Terrain	Apart from traverse of Glen Douchary and the path along the river which is rough going, the remainder is on excellent paths
Maps	OS Landranger 20 (Ben Dearg & Loch Broom); 16 (Lairg & Loch Shin): OS Explorer 436 (Beinn Dearg & Loch Fannich); 439 (Coigach & Summer Isles); 440 (Glen Cassley & Glen Oykel)
Amenities	Knockdamph bothy (NH 286 954); School House bothy (NH 340 975); hotel (Oykel Bridge)
Camping	Glen Douchary, Loch an Daimh, Glen Einig

As you zig-zag through the commercial pine plantation at Inverlael on wide paths, you could be forgiven for thinking this stage is going to be easy.

But after the travails of Glen Douchary, you may even find yourself calling an early halt to the day and stopping at the bothy at Knockdamph. If you continue, the paths are clear and good, becoming 4x4 tracks as you progress towards Oykel Bridge. There's another small bothy at Duag Bridge. Oykel Bridge is centred around the hotel.

Map continues on page 122

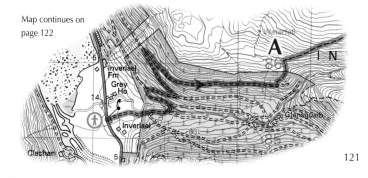

From **Inverlael**, turn right to leave the **A835** through the gate between a telephone box and a cottage. Proceed on the track, and pass through the gate into the forestry area. Bear left and cross the two bridges over the River Lael. After crossing the second bridge, turn left and climb through the forest on wide zig-zagging tracks. Pass through the gate to leave the forest and climb northeast on a reasonably clear path across the open hillside (**A**). From here the track becomes increasingly faint and boggy to a cairn around NH 225 875 (easily missed in poor visibility) (**B**).

The key from here is not to drop too far down towards **Allt na Lairige** – it's a horrible mess that will destroy your spirits early in the day. In low visibility, you'll need to be on your game with navigation as you contour and descend into **Glen Douchary**.

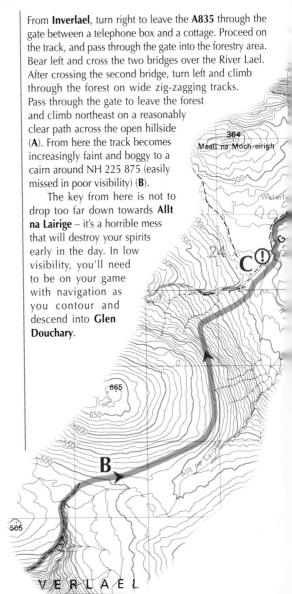

Mullach
a' Bhreun-Leitir
406

Map continues on
page 124

Glen Douchary
itself is stunningly
beautiful and much
of its flora and fauna
is unique. This makes it all
the more depressing that the
estate has chosen to carve an
ugly 4x4 track across the side of
one of Scotland's most beautiful glens.

Use the 520m contour as a guide
to skirt the hillside. The floor of the glen is
rough, so aim for the ruins at NH 244 901
(marked on OS 1:25,000 as sheepfolds) (**C**). You
should be able to cross the river relatively easily
here in normal conditions. ▶ After crossing the river,
follow the east bank of the river for 2.5km northeast

If the river is in
spate a crossing
here will probably
be impossible so
you'll need to drop
into the glen earlier,
descending along the
west bank of the Allt
na Lairige.

Rough ground above Inverlael Forest

123

The path, where it exists at all, is no more than a deer trail and progress is very rough and tiring.

Once you reach the loch, keep as close to the shore of the loch as possible, it's very wet and boggy here.

towards Loch an Daimh. ◄ As you approach the head of the gorge, contour northeast, there is no real path across the very rough grass and heather. Descend into a steep sided ravine, cross the **Allt nan Caorach** and then climb east northeast; there's no path and again the ground is rough. Head for the southwest end of **Loch an Daimh** (**D**). ◄ Climb to meet the main path above the loch at NH 260 938 (**E**), ignoring the lochside path which is rough and boggy. Once you reach the main

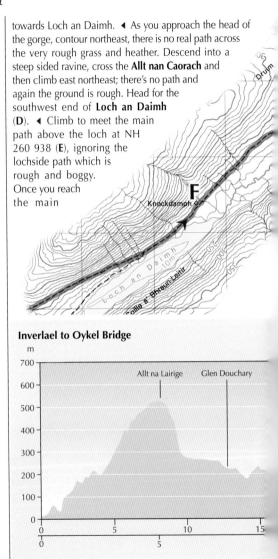

Inverlael to Oykel Bridge

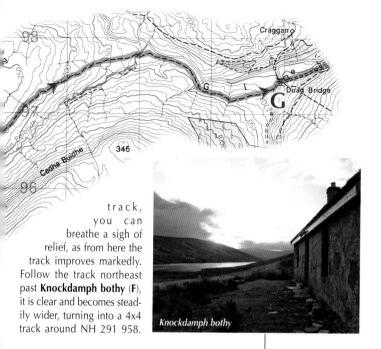

track, you can breathe a sigh of relief, as from here the track improves markedly. Follow the track northeast past **Knockdamph bothy** (**F**), it is clear and becomes steadily wider, turning into a 4x4 track around NH 291 958.

Knockdamph bothy

Map continues on page 126

Oykel Bridge

ft
2000
1500
1000
500
0

20   25   30   km
     15   20   miles

125

From here on the going is straightforward. Follow the 4x4 track to **Duag Bridge** where there is another bothy (**G**).

You may well be tempted to call it a day here.

◄ Climb gently from Duag bridge, taking the left hand fork in the track at NH 352 978.

Continue for 2km to another junction and after crossing the bridge at NH 367 984 (**H**) turn left and follow the 4x4 track which descends for 2km into **Oykel Bridge**, coming out onto a minor road and passing a row of houses before joining the main road.

Oykel Bridge Hotel is a rather upmarket place aimed at the huntin', shootin', fishin' crowd, but there are camping spots further up the river if it's out of your price range. There's also a post box as you descend pass a few houses to the main road. Bus and postbus services from Bonar Bridge to Ledmore and Lochinver pass through Oykel Bridge.

Route alternatives

If the weather is foul or your legs are suffering this is an easier alternative to an otherwise taxing stage.

If you visit Ullapool, Alternative Stage 9 below heads from the back of town towards Loch Achall and follows the Rhidorroch River to join the main route at Loch an Daimh. It's 4x4 tracks almost all the way and pleasant country. ◄

ALTERNATIVE STAGE 9

Ullapool to Oykel Bridge

Start	Ullapool
Finish	Oykel Bridge
Distance	30.9km (19¼ miles)
Ascent	330m
Average duration	1 day
Terrain	Easy walking on 4x4 tracks
Maps	OS Landranger 20 (Ben Dearg & Loch Broom); (19 Gairloch & Ullapool): OS Explorer 439 (Coigach & Summer Isles)
Amenities	Knockdamph bothy (NH 286 954)
Camping	Many lochside camping spots, if needed

If you divert to Ullapool, this stage provides a pleasant and easy way to rejoin the main route, without having to retrace your steps to Inverlael.

Take the A835 north out of Ullapool for about 1km. Just before you cross the Ullapool River, turn right onto a road signed Moorfield Quarry (**A**).
Continue east on this road for

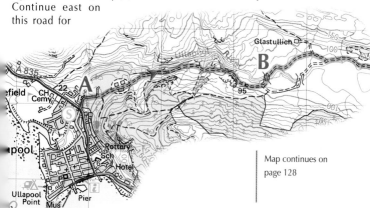

Map continues on page 128

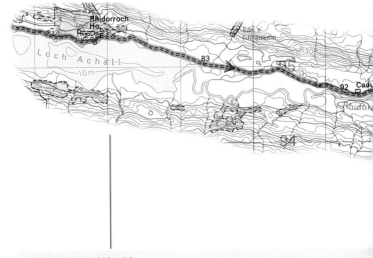

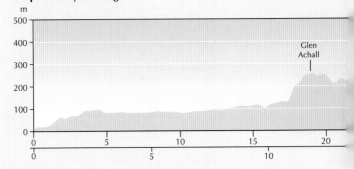

Ullapool to Oykel Bridge

For route directions
onwards to Duag
Bridge bothy and
Oykel Bridge,
see Stage 9 route
directions above.

2.5km past the quarry and descend to cross the **Ullapool River** (B). After crossing the river, take the 4x4 track that follows the north shore of **Loch Achall** for 3km. The track continues past Loch Achall and follows the **Rhidorroch River** for a further 7km before climbing **Glen Achall** past **East Rhidorroch Lodge** (C) and contouring for another 2km until **Loch an Daimh** comes into view. Follow the same track east to **Knockdamph** bothy where you rejoin the main route. ◀

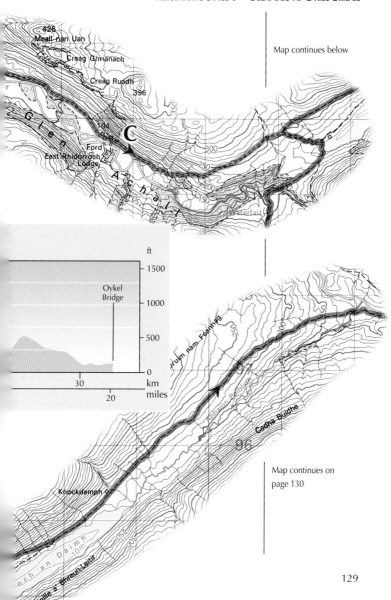

Map continues below

Map continues on
page 130

129

Map continues below

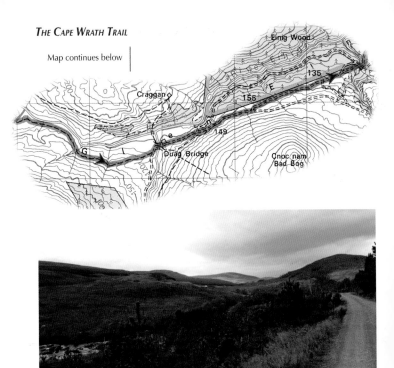

Wide tracks to Oykel Bridge

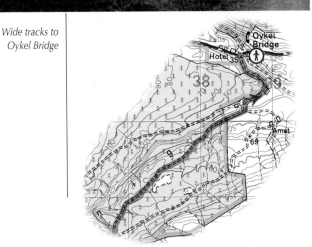

STAGE 10

Oykel Bridge to Inchnadamph (or Loch Ailsh)

Start	Oykel Bridge
Finish	Inchnadamph
Distance	29.9km (18½ miles)
Ascent	670m
Average duration	1–2 days
Terrain	Clear paths for most of the stage, with a short trackless section in upper Glen Oykel
Maps	OS Landranger 15 (Loch Assynt); 16 (Lairg & Loch Shin): OS Explorer 440 (Glen Cassley & Glen Oykel); 442 (Assynt & Lochinver)
Amenities	Hotel and hostel (Inchnadamph)
Camping	Great spots along the River Oykel, particularly beyond Loch Ailsh

The River Oykel is one of Scotland's finest salmon rivers, and from Oykel Bridge an excellent 4x4 track takes you all the way to Salachy. Fishing huts are dotted sporadically along the banks and on a sunny day this is a stunning place to be as the river tumbles elegantly over rocks and small waterfalls. From Salachy the path becomes a bit rougher as it hugs the river banks to Loch Ailsh and the splendidly located Benmore Lodge (a private hunting establishment). Walking north from here, you move onto the aprons of Ben More and Conival, two mountains connected by one of Scotland's finest ridges and often climbed together. You'll follow the River Oykel to its source and in the autumn, salmon return here to spawn, leaping out of the river from time to time.

There are some excellent wild camping spots, but as the track climbs towards Breabag Tarsainn, the ground becomes steadily rougher and in wild weather this is challenging country that should not be under-estimated.

Map continues on
page 134

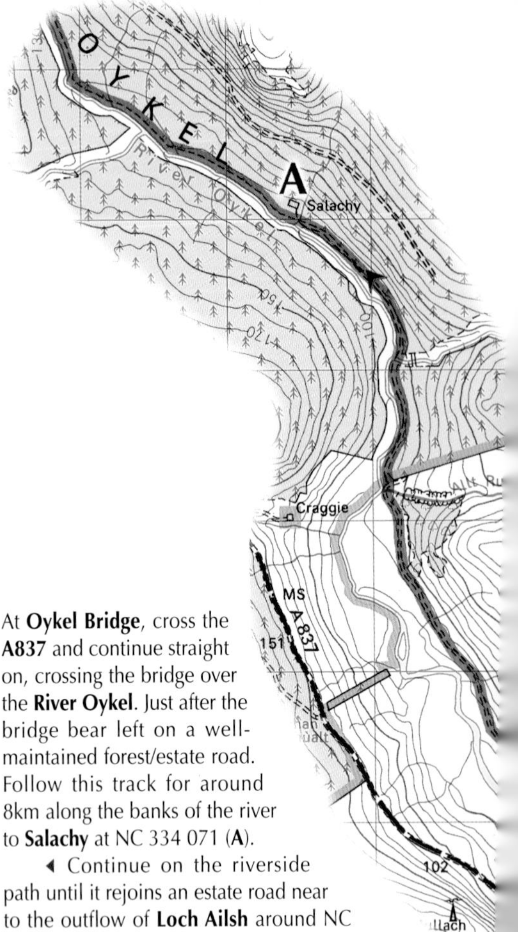

Salachy

Craggie

MS
A837
151

A837

102

llach
:hair

At **Oykel Bridge**, cross the
A837 and continue straight
on, crossing the bridge over
the **River Oykel**. Just after the
bridge bear left on a well-
maintained forest/estate road.
Follow this track for around
8km along the banks of the river
to **Salachy** at NC 334 071 (**A**).

From here the path
is clear to follow
along the banks of
the river but becomes
increasingly rough
and boggy.

◄ Continue on the riverside
path until it rejoins an estate road near
to the outflow of **Loch Ailsh** around NC
312 098 (**B**) and follow this estate road
north for 1.5km to **Benmore Lodge** (**C**). Pass
to the left of the lodge and continue on the
track for another 1.5km to the confluence of
rivers at NC 327 129 (**D**). There's a bridge here,
and once you've crossed it, continue north into
Glen Oykel on a clear path along the east river

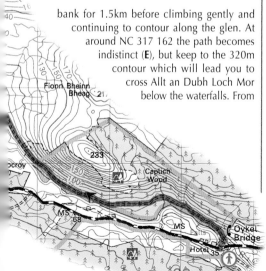

bank for 1.5km before climbing gently and continuing to contour along the glen. At around NC 317 162 the path becomes indistinct (**E**), but keep to the 320m contour which will lead you to cross Allt an Dubh Loch Mor below the waterfalls. From

Salmon fishing huts beside the River Oykel

133

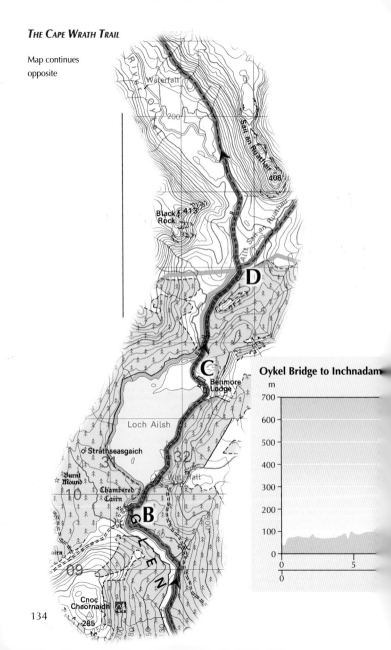

Oykel Bridge to Inchnadam

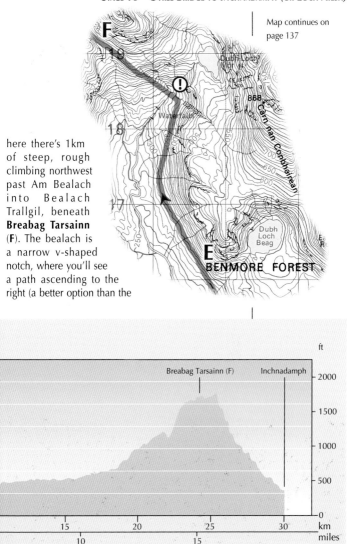

Map continues on page 137

here there's 1km of steep, rough climbing northwest past Am Bealach into Bealach Trallgil, beneath **Breabag Tarsainn** (**F**). The bealach is a narrow v-shaped notch, where you'll see a path ascending to the right (a better option than the

It's initially steep so take care on several awkward rock sections.

path that descends beside the river). Following the narrow, rocky path, descend from the bealach.

◄ As the slope lessens, the path peters out and crosses rough boggy ground for 1.5km northwest as you descend towards **Gleann Dubh**. Make for a crossing of

This could be another tricky crossing in spate.

the **River Traligill** around NC 286 203 (**G**). ◄

Once you've crossed the river follow an initially rough but clear path along the north bank which takes you the remaining 3km to **Inchnadamph**.

Descending to Inchnadamph

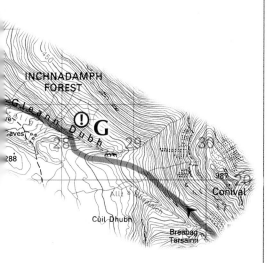

There's not much at Inchnadamph other than a cluster of houses, a hotel and a friendly hostel. At the time of writing a Postbus calls at Inchnadamph on its journey south to Lairg.

Route alternatives
The main route goes to Inchnadamph to take advantage of the amenities, but if the weather is fine then the route alternative via Gorm Loch Mòr (Alternative Stage 11) is splendidly isolated.

STAGE 11
Inchnadamph to Glendhu

Start	Inchnadamph
Finish	Glendhu via Glencoul
Distance	19.3km (12 miles)
Ascent	900m
Average duration	1 day
Terrain	Steep, rough, challenging terrain for the entire stage
Maps	OS Landranger 15 (Loch Assynt): OS Explorer 442 (Assynt & Lochinver)
Amenities	Glencoul bothy (NC 271 305); Glendhu bothy (NC 283 338)
Camping	By the lochs as you skirt Beinn Uidhe, shore of Loch Beag and Loch Glencoul

This stage is one of the hardest but finest of the whole trail, although in bad weather you'll need to have your wits about you. As you climb back out of Inchnadamph, skirting Cnoc an Droighinn, you're entering some of the best mountain country in the world. Crossing the corrie beneath Beinn Uidhe you climb steeply again to a pass between Glas Bheinn and Bheinn Uidhe before heading northeast towards the Was a Chual Aluinn waterfall. You'll definitely find it helpful to have an OS 1:25000 map for this section as route finding can be challenging, particularly in poor visibility. A rough, indistinct path takes you down to the potentially difficult river crossing of Abhainn an Loch Big which you follow to Loch Beag and onwards, skirting the coast to Glencoul where there is a fabulously located bothy (NC 271 305) that stares out towards Sail Ghorm and Sail Garbh.

By this stage you may be ready to call it a day, especially as the climb up from Glencoul around the Aird da Loch peninsula that juts into Loch Glencoul like the prow of a battleship is rough and taxing all the way to the bothy at Glendhu (NC 283 338).

From **Inchnadamph** climb northeast for 4km on a clear track that initially follows **Allt Poll an Droighinn** before climbing north to a path junction at NC 273 239. Take the left fork and continue north, skirting **Loch Fleodach Coire** (**A**) before ascending northwest to the Bealach na h-Uidhe pass below **Glas Bheinn** (**B**). From the bealach, descend northeast for 2km on a clear zig-zagging path to a small lochan at NC 279 269. Skirt the lochan and head briefly southeast looking out for a path junction at NC 281 268 (**C**). At this junction turn left – the path descends steeply at first and zig zags before contouring northwest to cross a burn. After crossing the burn the path

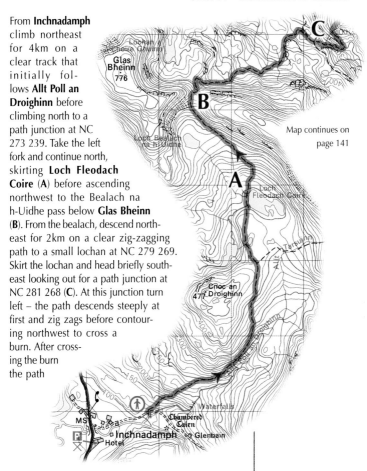

Map continues on
page 141

peters out, descend over steep, rough ground along the north side of the burn to the river **Abhainn an Loch Bhig**.

Cross the river where you can (this may be difficult in spate) and join a rough track on the north bank of the river. Follow the track 2km north to **Loch Beag** (**D**). After a kilometre or so, look out for the superb **Eas a Chual Aluinn**

139

waterfall to your west that cascades down towards the river. On reaching the loch, pick up another rough track along the coast, skirting inland around Torr na Coille to the bothy at **Glencoul** (**E**). From the bothy cross the footbridge and climb a rough track north-west, contouring around the **Aird da Loch** peninsula (**F**). ◄ As you round the penin-sula, the path is easy to lose, but becomes gradually clearer as you descend 2.5km towards Glendhu. The track comes out at the end of the loch where there is a footbridge over the river. Once you've crossed, turn left and follow the clear track 0.5km west to **Glendhu** bothy.

This is a steep, rough and tiring path.

Route alternatives

If you're feeling weary or want to steer closer to civilisation, you could follow the A894 north from Inchnadamph for a couple of kilometres

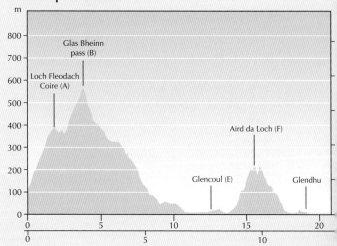

Inchnadamph to Glendhu

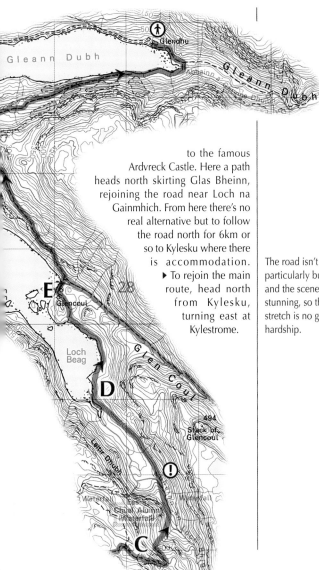

to the famous Ardvreck Castle. Here a path heads north skirting Glas Bheinn, rejoining the road near Loch na Gainmhich. From here there's no real alternative but to follow the road north for 6km or so to Kylesku where there is accommodation.

▶ To rejoin the main route, head north from Kylesku, turning east at Kylestrome.

The road isn't particularly busy and the scenery is stunning, so this stretch is no great hardship.

ALTERNATIVE STAGE 11
Loch Ailsh to Glendhu

Start	Ford beyond Loch Ailsh
Finish	Glendhu bothy
Distance	28.3km (17½ miles)
Ascent	630m
Duration	1 day
Terrain	Clear paths to start and finish with a very tough trackless middle section
Maps	OS Landranger 15 (Loch Assynt); 16 (Lairg & Loch Shin): OS Explorer 440 (Glen Cassley & Glen Oykel); 442 (Assynt & Lochinver)
Amenities	Glencoul bothy (NC 271 305)
Camping	Limited due to roughness of terrain

If you have no desire or need to head to civilisation at Inchnadamph, you have the option to continue northeast past Loch Ailsh via Loch Càrn nan Conbhairean, contouring around Ben More Assynt to Gorm Loch Mòr. From here a short but rough hack up and over to Loch an Eircill brings you to a path that you can follow all the way to rejoin the main route at Glencoul. This is all rough, challenging mountain country and on balance a harder alternative to the main route.

The steep-sided Aird da Loch peninsula overlooking Loch Glencoul

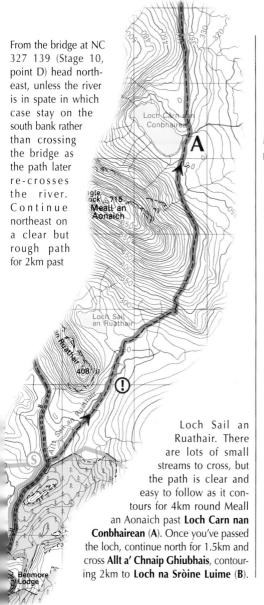

From the bridge at NC 327 139 (Stage 10, point D) head north-east, unless the river is in spate in which case stay on the south bank rather than crossing the bridge as the path later re-crosses the river. Continue northeast on a clear but rough path for 2km past

Map continues on page 144

Loch Sail an Ruathair. There are lots of small streams to cross, but the path is clear and easy to follow as it contours for 4km round Meall an Aonaich past **Loch Carn nan Conbhairean** (**A**). Once you've passed the loch, continue north for 1.5km and cross **Allt a' Chnaip Ghiubhais**, contouring 2km to **Loch na Sròine Luime** (**B**).

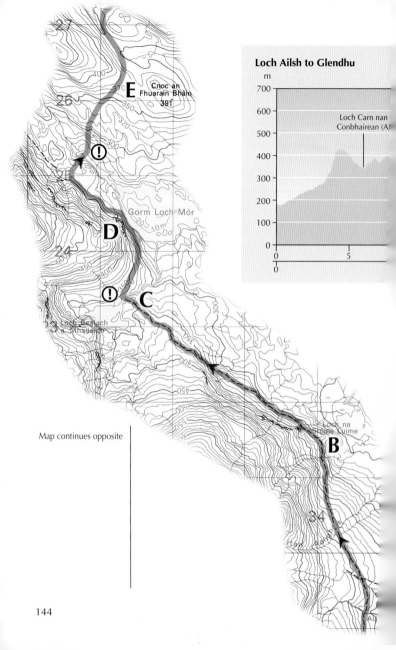

Loch Ailsh to Glendhu

Map continues opposite

144

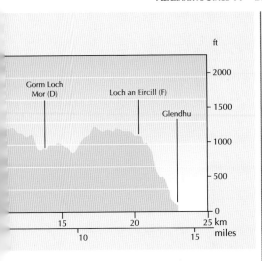

Continue past the loch, contouring northwest for 3km to **Loch Bealach a' Mhadaidh**, the path becomes increasingly rough and indistinct. At the loch cross the burn where it flows out of the loch (**C**) and contour north descending to the shore of Gorm Loch mor (**D**). ▶ Cross the river where

There's no path and as you follow the shore of Gorm Loch Mor northwest, the ground becomes increasingly rough.

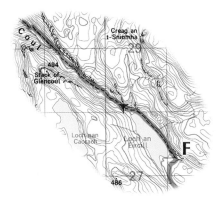

Map continues on page 146

145

To reach the beginning of Stage 12 follow the route description for Glencoul to Glendhu in Stage 11 above.

you can near Loch Suil Ceirsleich and climb for 1.5km over rough, trackless ground towards a broad pass beneath **Cnoc an Fhuarain Bhain** (**E**). From the pass descend over rough ground for 1.5km to pick up a track at the east end of **Loch an Eircill** (**F**). This track now leads you the remaining 5km to **Glencoul**, following the east shore of the loch and then descending along the east bank of the river, bringing you out near the bothy. ◄

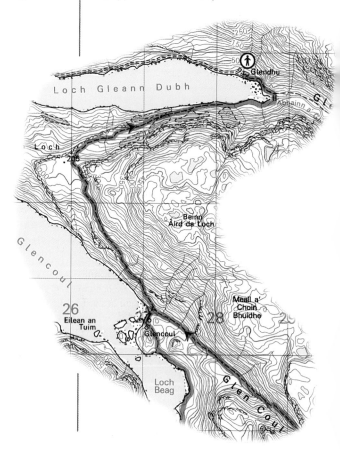

STAGE 12
Glendhu to Rhiconich

Start	Glendhu
Finish	Rhiconich
Distance	30.6km (19 miles)
Ascent	860m
Duration	1–2 days
Terrain	Initially good paths, but the second half of the stage is across almost entirely rough, boggy trackless ground
Maps	OS Landranger 15 (Loch Assynt); 9 (Cape Wrath, Durness & Scourie); OS Explorer 445 (Foinaven, Arkle, Kylesku & Scourie)
Amenities	Hotel (Rhiconich)
Camping	Ben Dreavie, upper Strath Stack, Loch Stack

Although the distance is not excessive, this is a tough stage to accomplish in a day, even for the fittest walkers. The majority of the route covers rough terrain, making progress slow and at times painful. The main route deliberately steers clear of the obvious road shortcut through Achfary, but no one would blame you for taking it as an alternative, although there are no amenities to be found in Achfary.

You leave Glendhu on a good loch side track, climbing to an ancient sheiling at Bealach nam Fiann. From here the path heads northwest over Ben Dreavie before descending via Loch na h-Ath, skirting the lower slopes of the stunning Ben Stack to the road at Lochstack lodge. The terrain is very rough, making walking difficult and tiring. The stretch after the lodge is initially on a good path but this gets increasingly rough and boggy until you reach Loch a'Garbh-bhaid Mòr. The river crossing at Garbh Allt can be difficult and dangerous so take great care. The final few kilometres into Rhiconich follow a clear path and you'll be glad to see the hotel at Rhiconich, if only for something recuperative in the warm bar. Buses from Kinlochbervie stop here.

From the bothy at **Glendhu** follow a clear lochside track 4km west to a path junction at NC 247 341 (**A**). Turn right and climb northeast for 2km, passing **Loch an Leithaid Bhuain**, before turning north for 0.75km to meet another clear track at NC 264 369 (**B**). Once you meet this track, turn right and head north for 2km to the **Shieling** at NC 272 384.

From here you have the choice whether to follow the main route or take the easier option via Achfary (see Route Alternatives below). The main route turns northwest from the Shieling (**C**) on a slightly less distinct path for 2km to the summit of **Ben Dreavie** (**D**). From Ben Dreavie descend

Map continues opposite

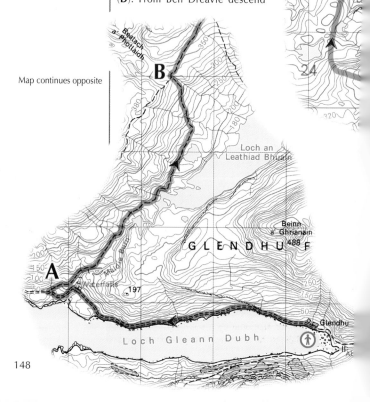

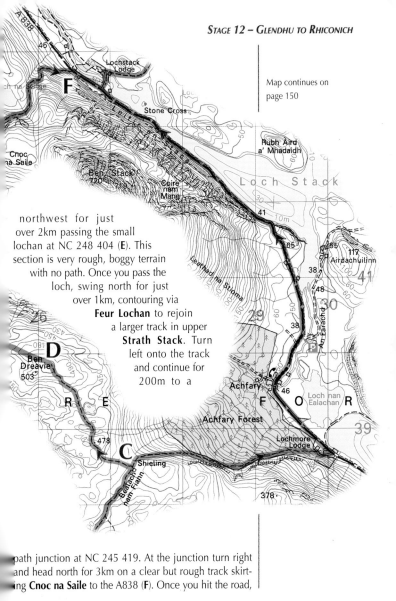

Map continues on
page 150

northwest for just
over 2km passing the small
lochan at NC 248 404 (**E**). This
section is very rough, boggy terrain
with no path. Once you pass the
loch, swing north for just
over 1km, contouring via
Feur Lochan to rejoin
a larger track in upper
Strath Stack. Turn
left onto the track
and continue for
200m to a

path junction at NC 245 419. At the junction turn right
and head north for 3km on a clear but rough track skirting **Cnoc na Saile** to the A838 (**F**). Once you hit the road,

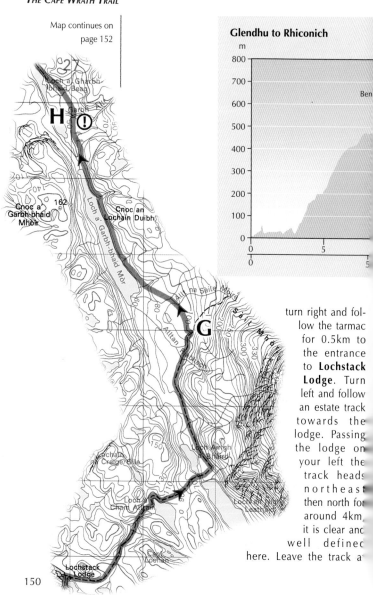

Map continues on
page 152

Glendhu to Rhiconich

turn right and fol-
low the tarmac
for 0.5km to
the entrance
to **Lochstack
Lodge**. Turn
left and follow
an estate track
towards the
lodge. Passing
the lodge on
your left the
track heads
northeast
then north for
around 4km,
it is clear and
well defined
here. Leave the track a

150

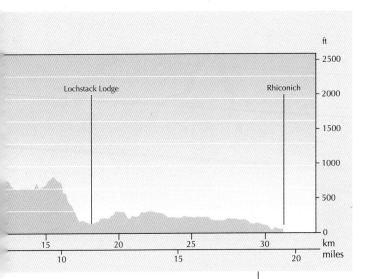

NC 286 469 (**G**), shortly after crossing the Allt an Riabhach and head northwest for 1km across rough ground. ▸ Once you reach the head of **Loch a' Garbh-bhaid Mòr**, keep to its east bank. There is a vague path, but again it is very rough and boggy. Continue for 2km along the east side of the loch and then a further kilometre to the **Garbh Allt** (**H**).

There's no path here and it's rocky and boggy.

> This is a **difficult river crossing** and may be impassable in spate. There is a small braid 0.5km inland from the loch which is generally the easiest place to cross.

Once you've successfully negotiated the river, you will pick up a slightly better path along the shore of **Loch a' Garbh-bhaid Beag** (**I**) that takes you the remaining 3km to **Rhiconich**, improving gradually as it goes.

Route alternatives
The main route deliberately avoids the road, so for an easier alternative, descend from Bealach nam Fiann

Achfary Forest with Arkle in the background

(NC 273 385) skirting through Achfary Forest to the A838. Passing through Achfary (no amenities to detain you here) you can then follow the road northwest all the way to Lochstack Lodge. This far north, the road isn't that busy. If you prefer to avoid roads, but still want to shave some distance and difficulty, there is another alternative route beside Loch Stack. Leave Achfary on the A838 towards Laxford Bridge and after about a kilometre take the track at NC 297 402. Continue on the track crossing the river at Lone via a bridge before turning north northwest, heading for the shore of Loch Stack. Follow the shore before ascending slowly to join the main route around NC 287 459.

STAGE 13
Rhiconich to Sandwood Bay

Start	Rhiconich
Finish	Sandwood Bay
Distance	16.2km (10 miles)
Ascent	350m
Average duration	1 day
Terrain	Road to Badcall, rough, mainly trackless terrain to Sandwood Bay
Maps	OS Landranger 9 (Cape Wrath): OS Explorer 446 (Durness & Cape Wrath)
Amenities	Shop (London Stores, Badcall); Strathan Bothy (NC 247 612); hotel, B&B, shop, Post Office (Kinlochbervie); Strathchailleach bothy (NC 249 657)
Camping	Strathan, Sandwood Bay

The B801 north from Rhiconich along the shore of Loch Inchard is not a busy road, but the locals have a tendency to negotiate its twists and turns at breakneck speed and there are also large lorries servicing the port at Kinlochbervie, so take care. From Badcall the main route heads due north via the bothy at Strathan. There's something quite special about knowing so few humans pass this way. From Strathan the going doesn't get much easier as you follow the edge of Sandwood loch to the majestic Sandwood Bay.

After crossing so much difficult ground, the cross country route from Badcall is suggested from the point of view of road-avoiding purism. However many walkers will quite understandably want to divert to take advantage of the amenities in Kinlochbervie (see below). The alternative route to Sandwood Bay from Kinlochbervie via Blairmore arguably provides a better view as you descend to Sandwood Bay. It's your call.

From the Rhiconich **Hotel**, take the left fork in the road and follow the **B801** for 4km almost all the way to **Badcall** (**A**). Look for a 4x4 track at NC 241 557.

The **London Stores**, about 50m further up the road from here, is a Cape Wrath Trail institution. Almost everything imaginable is crammed into a tiny Aladdin's cave of a shop. The shop may also hold postal re-supply packages for you if you phone and ask nicely.

This is rough, trackless, leg sapping terrain, but beautiful in its own way.

Turn right and follow the track for about 1km northwest. As the track ends, head north and climb across rough, trackless country for 3km towards **Meall Dearg** (**B**) at NC 246 593. ◀ Contour round Meall Dearg and descend for 2km, skirting Lochan a Chombaiste towards **Strathan** (**C**), crossing the river via the footbridge at NC 244 610. From the bothy, take a very rough track northwest: the track is difficult to follow and soon peters out. Continue heading northwest for 3km along **Strath Shinary** to **Sandwood Loch** (**D**).

There's no path and the ground is very rough, with several crossings of small burns that run into the loch.

Once you reach the loch, follow the northeast shore. ◀ Although it's only another 2km to Sandwood Bay, this section is tough. You'll come out at the northeastern end of Sandwood Bay.

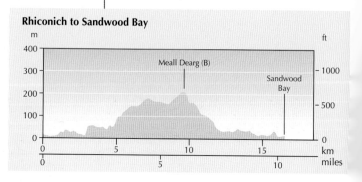

Rhiconich to Sandwood Bay

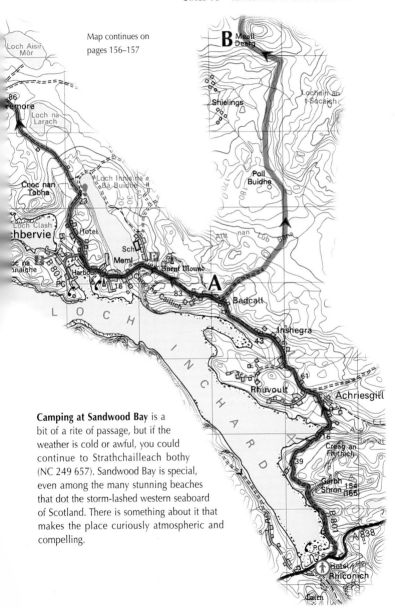

Map continues on pages 156–157

Camping at Sandwood Bay is a bit of a rite of passage, but if the weather is cold or awful, you could continue to Strathchailleach bothy (NC 249 657). Sandwood Bay is special, even among the many stunning beaches that dot the storm-lashed western seaboard of Scotland. There is something about it that makes the place curiously atmospheric and compelling.

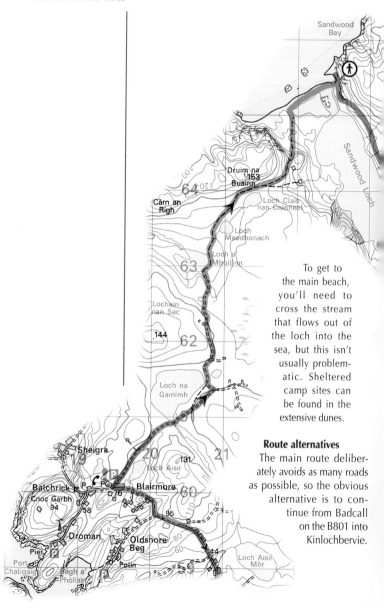

To get to the main beach, you'll need to cross the stream that flows out of the loch into the sea, but this isn't usually problematic. Sheltered camp sites can be found in the extensive dunes.

Route alternatives

The main route deliberately avoids as many roads as possible, so the obvious alternative is to continue from Badcall on the B801 into Kinlochbervie.

Kinlochbervie is a year round fishing port and so has more amenities than you'd expect this far north, even in the off season: a hotel, B&Bs, Post Office and small shop selling supplies.

From Kinlochbervie, follow the road north via Oldshoremore to Blairmore. Houses are strung out here and there along the road, built end on to the coast – testament to the raw power of the elements. From Blairmore, a clear 4x4 track track strikes out northeast for 6km over the moors skirting four lochans before delivering you to an awe inspiring vista of Sandwood Bay. ▶

Rowing boat near Sandwood Loch

If conditions are clear, you'll catch your first and only glimpse of the lighthouse at the cape here – you won't see it again until you're almost upon it.

157

STAGE 14
Sandwood Bay to Cape Wrath

Start	Sandwood Bay
Finish	Cape Wrath
Distance	12.9km (8 miles)
Ascent	330m
Average duration	1 day
Terrain	Rough, boggy, trackless ground all the way
Maps	OS Landranger 9 (Cape Wrath): OS Explorer 446 (Durness & Cape Wrath)
Amenities	Ozone Café (Cape Wrath); Kearvaig bothy (NC 292 727)
Camping	Rough, boggy ground so you'll have to choose carefully: there's a good spot around NC 259 728

The last stage of your journey to Cape Wrath can feel like one of the hardest. Beyond Sandwood Bay it's a slog across beautiful but bleak, peat-dark rolling moors, with the North Atlantic often throwing its worst at you. It's tough going at times and completely trackless, but the remoteness is intoxicating. It's a day you'll remember, especially when the lighthouse finally peeks into view as you round the final hill. The last section of land to the cape itself is part of the Cape Wrath Ministry of Defence (MOD) live firing range. You'll need to check in advance if any range activity is planned during your visit. Activity on the range is usually advertised in advance, call range control on 0800 833 300 or 01971 511242 for more information. There is almost no mobile phone reception on Cape Wrath so all telephone arrangements or enquiries must be made in advance.

There is nothing much at Cape Wrath other than the jagged beauty of the towering sea cliffs, the lighthouse itself and a clump of mostly abandoned buildings. A hardy entrepreneur, John Ure, runs the Ozone Café, which is open all year round. What sounds at first like a local joke at the expense of visitors turns out to be true, and a warm cup of tea, soup, sandwiches and snacks can be had in the company of a large pack of springer spaniels. The café also provides basic overnight accommodation with a cooked breakfast (call in advance if you're planning to stay, 01971 511314).

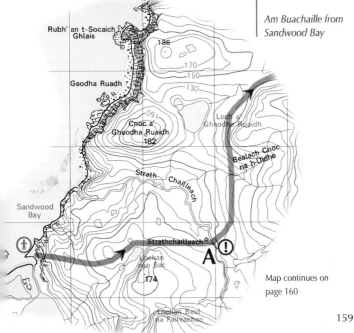

Am Buachaille from Sandwood Bay

Map continues on page 160

159

Map continues on
page 162

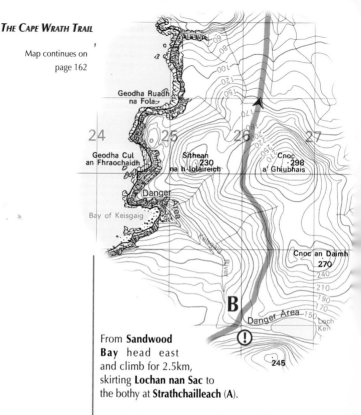

From **Sandwood Bay** head east and climb for 2.5km, skirting **Lochan nan Sac** to the bothy at **Strathchailleach** (**A**).

Even if you're not intending to stay, it's worth poking your head in. The bothy was home to **James McRory-Smith** (also known as Sandy) for 40 years. He lived the life of a hermit with no gas, electricity or telephone, making only occasional journeys to the London Stores in Badcall to collect his pension and stock up on food. His atmospheric paintings still adorn the walls.

Cross the river at the bothy with care, this will be difficult in spate. Once you've negotiated the river, head north for 2km following the contours of the shallow hills that abut the coast to the Keisgaig River. ◀ Once you've

The ground is rough, boggy and trackless.

crossed the **Keisgaig River** (**B**) (potentially difficult in spate) you'll soon encounter the barbed wire fence that delineates the MOD range boundary. Climb the fence with care and head almost due north for 2km, contouring around **Cnoca a' Ghiubhais**. From here descend north for 2.5km, passing some old shielings before a short climb to meet a 4x4 track at NC 264 731 (**C**). Turn left and follow the 4x4 track for 2km to the **Cape Wrath** lighthouse.

Cape Wrath lighthouse (photo: David Wilson)

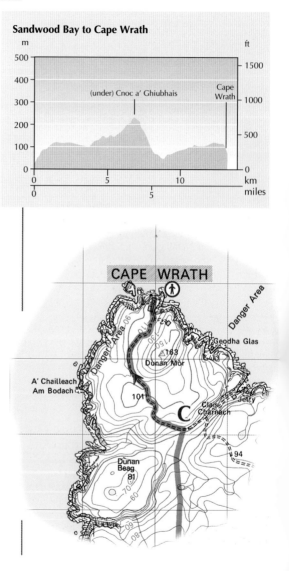

Sandwood Bay to Cape Wrath

CAPE WRATH

A barbed wire fence marking the southern range boundary is encountered soon after crossing the Keisgaig River. Red flags fly and warning notices are posted when the range is in use. Some walkers have reported finding red flags flying, despite being told in advance that there would be no range activity. There is some suspicion that this is because the MOD finds it easier to leave flags flying than travel out to take them down. Needless to say it has been pointed out to the MOD that such behaviour destroys the deterrent value of the flags and contravenes their responsibility for managing access to the cape, but at the time of writing the issue has yet to be properly resolved. Live, inert or expended ammunition may be found on the range, so if you come across a suspicious object, leave it alone and contact range control with a grid reference and description on your return.

The cape itself marks the angle where the Viking ships altered course, veering south to enter The Minch on their way to the West coast of Scotland and the Hebrides (its name is derived from the old Norse name for Cape Wrath, 'Hvarf' or 'turning-point'). Standing on Cape Wrath, you are at 122 metres above the waves, on some of the highest cliffs in the UK. Some way to the east is Dunnet Head, the most northerly point of mainland Britain (not John o'Groats as is commonly supposed). North, there's nothing between you and the North Pole some 2,700km away. Once you reach the cape, you'll finally see the lighthouse you've probably imagined in your thoughts for some time. The light was built in 1827 and can be seen for 40km. The now silent foghorn once boomed mournfully into the North Atlantic to warn passing ships of the dangers lurking around the jagged sea cliffs. These days the light is surrounded by a clump of mostly abandoned buildings, gradually surrendering to the fierce sea winds.

If you're not staying at the café, the buildings at the cape are not the most pleasant place to camp. They have an eerie, deserted feeling as the wind whistles between them. If you're intending to camp, you may prefer to retrace your steps to NC 259 728 which is a sheltered and pleasant spot. There is also the superbly located Kearvaig bothy 10km or so to the east of the cape. When the time comes to leave, refer to 'Access to and return from Cape Wrath' under 'Getting around'.

Looking towards the cape, Sandwood Bay

EPILOGUE

At the end of such an epic journey, as you wander through the slightly forlorn buildings hunched on the wind-seared cliffs of the cape, it's only natural to have mixed feelings. Elation at having reached your final objective, satisfaction at having endured the physical hardships along the way, humility in the face of the raw power of nature all around, regret or relief that the journey is finally over.

It will take days if not weeks to process the magnitude of this experience, but as you float across the Kyle of Durness or retrace your steps to Kinlochbervie, it's worth reflecting on the words of John Muir, written more than a century ago, but still remarkably prescient:

> Thousands of tired, nerve-shaken, over-civilized people are
> beginning to find out that going to the mountains is going home;
> that wildness is a necessity.

It's easy to get sucked back into the hectic pell-mell of everyday life, leaving trail memories distant, detached and unreal. But try to hold on to some of the sedate pace of the wilderness, remembering the simple pleasures of getting from one place to another, surviving and traversing a landscape that has existed since time immemorial.

The cape will still be standing, stolid and immovable, a giant buttress to the wild atlantic, long after our own time has come and gone. And you were there, in that place and in that moment.

APPENDIX A
Route summary table

Section	Stage	Title	Distance	Duration
1	1	Fort William to Glenfinnan	34.3km (21¼ miles)	1–2 days
	2	Glenfinnan to Glen Dessarry	18.1km (11¼ miles)	1 day
	3	Glen Dessarry to Barisdale	24.8km (15½ miles)	1–2 days
	4	Barisdale to Morvich (near Shiel Bridge)	31.5km (19½ miles)	2 days
	alt 1	Fort William to Laggan	41km (25½ miles)	1–2 days
	alt 2	Laggan to Cluanie	44.7km (27¾ miles)	1–2 days
	alt 3	Cluanie to Morvich (near Shiel Bridge)	26.6km (16½ miles)	1–2 days
	5	Morvich (near Shiel Bridge) to Strathcarron (see also Alternative Stage 6)	38.7km (24 miles)	2 days
2	6	Strathcarron to Kinlochewe	34.7km (21½ miles)	1–2 days
	alt 6	Bendronaig to Kinlochewe	37.8km (23½ miles)	1–2 days
	7	Kinlochewe to Strath na Sealga	27.3km (17 miles)	1 day
	8	Strath na Sealga to Inverlael (near Ullapool)	18.2km (11¼ miles)	1 day
3	9	Inverlael to Oykel Bridge	33.5km (20¾ miles)	1–2 days
	alt 9	Ullapool to Oykel Bridge	30.9km (19¼ miles)	1–2 days
	10	Oykel Bridge to Inchnadamph (see also Alternative Stage 11)	29.9km (18½ miles)	1 day
	11	Inchnadamph to Glendhu	19.3km (12 miles)	1 day
	alt 11	Loch Ailsh to Glendhu	28.8km (12½ miles)	1–2 days
	12	Glendhu to Rhiconich	30.6km (19 miles)	1–2 days
	13	Rhiconich to Sandwood Bay	16.2km (10 miles)	1 day
	14	Sandwood Bay to Cape Wrath	12.9km (8 miles)	1 day
		Total (main route only)	**370km (231¼ miles)**	**16–21 days**

APPENDIX B
Accommodation

The accommodation listed here is not fully comprehensive and for larger settlements it is impractical for to list accommodation available. Remoter accommodation may only open for part of the year (typically April–October), so always check and book in advance.

Please see http://www.capewrathtrailguide.org/accommodation for up-to-date contact details and web links.

Section 1

Stages 1–4

Fort William
Fort William Backpackers
Numerous B&Bs & hotels

Glenfinnan
Prince's House Hotel
Glenfinnan House Hotel
Glenfinnan Sleeping Car Bunkhouse
Corryhully Bothy (NM 912 844)
A'Chùil Bothy (NM 944 924)
Sourlies Bothy (NM 869 951)

Barisdale
Campsite, bothy, self-catering

Kinloch Hourn
Kinloch Hourn Farm B&B

Shiel Bridge
Campsites, hotel, bunkhouse, B&Bs

Morvich
Campsite

Ratagan
Youth hostel

Alternative Stages 1–3

Banavie
Chase the Wild Goose Hostel

Gairlochy
Dalcomera B&B

Laggan
Great Glen Hostel
Forest Lodge B&B

Invergarry
Invergarry Hotel
Faichemard Farm Campsite
B&Bs

Cluanie
Cluanie Inn Hotel
Alltbeithe Youth Hostel
Camban Bothy (NH 053 184)

Shiel Bridge
Campsites, hotel, bunkhouse, B&Bs

Morvich
Campsite

Stage 5
Maol Bhuidhe Bothy (NH 052 360)
Bendroniag Lodge Bothy (NH 014 389)
Strathcarron Hotel

Section 2

Stage 6
Coire Fionnaraich bothy (NG 950 480)
Torridon Youth Hostel

Kinlochewe
Hotel, bunkhouse, B&Bs
Taggan campsite (NH 014 636)

Alternative Stage 6
Bernais Bothy (NH 021 431)
Easan Dorcha Bothy (NH 012 526)
Gerry's Hostel, Achnashellach

Kinlochewe
Hotel, bunkhouse, B&Bs, campsite

Stage 7
Leckie Bothy (NH 096 645)
Shenavall Bothy (NH 066 810)

Stage 8

Dundonnell
The Dundonnell Hotel
Sail Mhor Croft Hostel
B&Bs

Inverlael
B&Bs

Ullapool
Numerous hotels, B&Bs, hostels

Section 3

Stage 9
Knockdamph Bothy (NH 286 954)
School House bothy (NH 340 975)
Oykel Bridge Hotel

Stage 10
Inchnadamph Hotel
Inchnadamph Lodge Hostel

Stage 11
Glencoul Bothy (NC 271 305)
Glendhu Bothy (NC 283 338)

Stage 12
Rhiconich Hotel

Stage 13
Strathan Bothy (NC 247 612)

Kinlochbervie
Hotel, B&Bs

Stage 14
Strathchailleach Bothy (NC 249 657)
The Ozone café
Kearvaig Bothy (NC 292 727)

Durness
B&Bs, hostel, bunkhouse, campsite

APPENDIX C
Shops, cafés and Post Offices

Re-supply along the trail is a challenge due to the general remoteness and lack of amenities. Any amenities available are listed below by nearest town, south to north.

Fort William
Large Morrisons supermarket
Several outdoor stores
Post Office

Laggan (on alternative route)
Seven Heads Store, Invergarry,
By Spean Bridge, 01809 501246

Shiel Bridge
Small shop at petrol station

Achnashellach
Café at station

Kinlochewe
Shop and Post Office
Small shop at petrol station
Whistlestop Café, Old Village Hall

Ullapool
Large Tesco supermarket
North West Outdoors
Cafés
Post Office
Laundromat (opposite Tesco)

Inchnadamph
Limited supplies can be purchased from the Inchnadamph Lodge hostel (check availability in advance 01571 822218)

Kinlochbervie
London Stores, Badcall, 01971 521273
Small Spar supermarket (at harbour)
Post Office

Cape Wrath
Ozone Café, Cape Wrath Lighthouse, 01971 511314

Durness
Small Spar supermarket
Post Office

APPENDIX D
Useful websites

Travel

Traveline Scotland
www.travelinescotland.com

Camusnagaul ferry (Fort William)
www.lochabertransport.org.uk

Cape Wrath information
www.capewrath.org.uk

Scotrail
www.scotrail.co.uk

Royal Mail post bus service
www.royalmail.com

Cape Wrath Ferry
www.capewrathferry.co.uk

Accommodation

www.capewrathtrailguide.org/
accommodation

UK Bothies forums
ukbothies.freeforums.org

Tripadvisor
www.tripadvisor.co.uk

Mountain Bothy Association (MBA)
www.mountainbothies.org.uk

Scottish Youth Hostel Association
www.syha.org.uk

Visit Scotland
www.visitscotland.com

Access

General access information
www.outdooraccess-scotland.com

Deer stalking information
www.snh.org.uk/hillphones

Wild camping
www.mcofs.org.uk/assets/pdfs/
wildcamping.pdf

Miscellaneous

Midge forecast
www.midgeforecast.co.uk

The Mountaineering Council
of Scotland
www.mcofs.org.uk

BMC Hill Skills
www.thebmc.co.uk

Mountain Weather Information Service
www.mwis.org.uk

MOD range at Cape Wrath
www.mod.uk

APPENDIX E

Maps

**Ordnance Survey Landranger
(1:50,000 scale)**

41   Ben Nevis
40   Mallaig & Glenfinnan
34   Fort Augustus (Alternative Stage 1)
33   Loch Alsh & Glen Shiel
25   Glen Carron & Glen Affric
20   Ben Dearg & Loch Broom
19   Gairloch & Ullapool
15   Loch Assynt
16   Lairg & Loch Shin
(9   Cape Wrath, Durness & Scourie)

**Ordnance Survey Explorer
(1:25,000 scale)**

391 Ardgour & Strontian
392 Ben Nevis & Fort William
398 Loch Morar & Mallaig
400 Loch Lochy & Glen Roy
413 Knoydart, Loch Hourn & Loch
     Duich
414 Glen Shiel & Kintail Forest
415 Glen Affric & Glen Morriston

429 Glen Carron & West Monar
433 Torridon, Beinn Eighe & Liathach
435 An Teallach & Slioch
436 Beinn Dearg & Loch Fannich
439 Coigach & Summer Isles
440 Glen Cassley & Glen Oykel
442 Assynt & Lochinver
445 Foinaven, Arkle, Kylesku & Scourie
446 Durness & Cape Wrath

**Harvey British Mountain Map
(1:40,000 scale)**

Knoydart, Kintail and Glen Affric

**Harvey Superwalker
(1:25,000 scale)**

Torridon

Kintail (Glen Shiel)

Suilven

APPENDIX F
Further reading

---

*Hostile Habitats – Scotland's Mountain
Environment: A Hillwalkers' Guide to
Wildlife and the Landscape*
Mark Wrightam and Nick Kempe
(2006)

*Hutton's Arse: 3 Billion Years of
Extraordinary Geology in Scotland's
Northern Highlands*
Malcolm Rider (2005)

Scotland (World Mountain Ranges)
Chris Townsend (Cicerone 2010)

*A Light in the Wilderness:
The History of Cape Wrath*
David Hird (Balnakeil Press 2008)

*The Cape Wrath Trail.
A 200-mile walk through the North-
West Scottish Highlands*
David Paterson (1996)

*Cape Wrath to Brora.
A walking adventure across Sutherland*
Nick Lindsay (Sunnybrae press 2010)

LISTING OF CICERONE GUIDES

Tour of the Oisans: The GR54
Tour of the Queyras
Tour of the Vanoise
Trekking in the Vosges and Jura
Vanoise Ski Touring
Walking in Provence
Walking in the Auvergne
Walking in the Cathar Region
Walking in the Cevennes
Walking in the Dordogne
Walking in the Haute Savoie
  North & South
Walking in the Languedoc
Walking in the Tarentaise and
  Beaufortain Alps
Walking on Corsica

GERMANY
Germany's Romantic Road
Walking in the Bavarian Alps
Walking in the Harz Mountains
Walking the River Rhine Trail

HIMALAYA
Annapurna
Bhutan
Everest: A Trekker's Guide
Garhwal and Kumaon:
  A Trekker's and
  Visitor's Guide
Kangchenjunga:
  A Trekker's Guide
Langtang with Gosainkund
  and Helambu:
  A Trekker's Guide
Manaslu: A Trekker's Guide
The Mount Kailash Trek
Trekking in Ladakh

ICELAND AND GREENLAND
Trekking in Greenland
Walking and Trekking in
  Iceland

IRELAND
Irish Coastal Walks
The Irish Coast to Coast Walk
The Mountains of Ireland

ITALY
Gran Paradiso
Italy's Sibillini National Park
Shorter Walks in the Dolomites
Through the Italian Alps

Trekking in the Apennines
Trekking in the Dolomites
Via Ferratas of the Italian
  Dolomites: Vols 1 & 2
Walking in Abruzzo
Walking in Sardinia
Walking in Sicily
Walking in the Central
  Italian Alps
Walking in the Dolomites
Walking in Tuscany
Walking on the Amalfi Coast
Walking the Italian Lakes

MEDITERRANEAN
Jordan – Walks, Treks, Caves,
  Climbs and Canyons
The Ala Dag
The High Mountains of Crete
The Mountains of Greece
Treks and Climbs in
  Wadi Rum, Jordan
Walking in Malta
Western Crete

NORTH AMERICA
British Columbia
The Grand Canyon
The John Muir Trail
The Pacific Crest Trail

SOUTH AMERICA
Aconcagua and the
  Southern Andes
Torres del Paine

SCANDINAVIA
Walking in Norway

SLOVENIA, CROATIA
AND MONTENEGRO
The Julian Alps of Slovenia
The Mountains of Montenegro
Trekking in Slovenia
Walking in Croatia
Walking in the Karavanke

SPAIN AND PORTUGAL
Costa Blanca: West
Mountain Walking in
  Southern Catalunya
The Mountains of Central Spain
The Northern Caminos
Trekking through Mallorca

Walking in Madeira
Walking in Mallorca
Walking in the Algarve
Walking in the
  Cordillera Cantabrica
Walking in the Sierra Nevada
Walking on La Gomera and
  El Hierro
Walking on La Palma
Walking on Tenerife
Walks and Climbs in
  the Picos de Europa

SWITZERLAND
Alpine Pass Route
Canyoning in the Alps
Central Switzerland
The Bernese Alps
The Swiss Alps
Tour of the Jungfrau Region
Walking in the Valais
Walking in Ticino
Walks in the Engadine

TECHNIQUES
Geocaching in the UK
Indoor Climbing
Lightweight Camping
Map and Compass
Mountain Weather
Moveable Feasts
Outdoor Photography
Polar Exploration
Rock Climbing
Sport Climbing
The Book of the Bivvy
The Hillwalker's Guide
  to Mountaineering
The Hillwalker's Manual

MINI GUIDES
Avalanche!
Navigating with a GPS
Navigation
Pocket First Aid and Wilderness
  Medicine
Snow

For full information on all
our guides, and to order
books and eBooks, visit our
website: **www.cicerone.co.uk**.

Walking – Trekking – Mountaineering – Climbing – Cycling

Over 40 years, Cicerone have built up an outstanding collection of 300 guides, inspiring all sorts of amazing adventures.

Every guide comes from extensive exploration and research by our expert authors, all with a passion for their subjects. They are frequently praised, endorsed and used by clubs, instructors and outdoor organisations.

All our titles can now be bought as **e-books** and many as iPad and Kindle files and we will continue to make all our guides available for these and many other devices.

Our website shows any **new information** we've received since a book was published. Please do let us know if you find anything has changed, so that we can pass on the latest details. On our **website** you'll also find some great ideas and lots of information, including sample chapters, contents lists, reviews, articles and a photo gallery.

It's easy to keep in touch with what's going on at Cicerone, by getting our monthly **free e-newsletter**, which is full of offers, competitions, up-to-date information and topical articles. You can subscribe on our home page and also follow us on **Facebook** and **Twitter**, as well as our **blog**.

Cicerone – the very best guides for exploring the world.

CICERONE

2 Police Square Milnthorpe Cumbria LA7 7PY
Tel: 015395 62069 info@cicerone.co.uk
www.cicerone.co.uk